Volume I

Study Guide

John Moretta
Houston Community College, Central College

Susan Hult
Houston Community College, Central College

Western Civilization
The Continuing Experiment

Thomas F. X. Noble
University of Virginia

Barry S. Strauss
Cornell University

Duane J. Osheim
University of Virginia

Kristen B. Neuschel
Duke University

William B. Cohen
Indiana University

David D. Roberts
University of Georgia

HOUGHTON MIFFLIN COMPANY   BOSTON   TORONTO
Geneva, Illinois   Palo Alto   Princeton, New Jersey

Sponsoring Editor: Sean Wakely
Basic Book Editor: Elizabeth M. Welch
Editorial Assistant: Stefanie Jacobs
Production Coordinator: LuAnn Belmonte Paladino
Senior Manufacturing Coordinator: Marie Barnes
Marketing Manager: Rebecca J. Dudley

Printed in the U.S.A.

ISBN: 0-395-55127-7

123456789-CS-98 97 96 95 94

CONTENTS

This Study Guide was designed to help you master the material in *Western Civilization: The Continuing Experiment* by Thomas Noble, Barry Strauss, Duane Osheim, Kristen Neuschel, William Cohen, and David Roberts. The Study Guide supplements the text but does not replace it. If used properly, it should help you to understand and master key facts, concepts, and issues discussed in the text.

Each Study Guide chapter corresponds to a text chapter and contains a list of Learning Objectives, a Summary of the chapter, 8 to 10 Multiple-Choice Questions with answers for self-checking, 10 to 15 Terms for Identification, 3 to 5 Short-Answer and Essay Questions, and 1 to 4 Map Exercises that should enhance your geographical knowledge. Answer Guidelines for the Short-Answer Questions appear at the end of the book.

We hope you find this Study Guide helpful in your study of western civilization.

The Ancestors of the West

Learning Objectives

After studying this chapter, you should be able to:

1. trace the changes in human being's predecessors from *Homo erectus* to *Homo sapiens*.

2. understand the evolving human activities that led to civilization.

3. analyze the complex institutions and pressures that composed Mesopotamian society.

4. discuss how the Sumerian city-states arose.

5. analyze the conquest of Sumerian city-states by the Akkadians and the assimilation that was their lasting legacy.

6. understand Egypt's unique contributions to Western religion, politics, arts, and science.

7. discuss the characteristics of the city-states in Syria-Palestine and the Hittites' rise.

Summary

The first modern human beings evolved from their humanlike ancestors sometime between 200,000 and 40,000 years ago. Their earliest ancestors had appeared in the African tropics and subtropics nearly 5 million years ago. About 1.6 million years ago they had transformed into the humanlike ancestor known as *Homo erectus*, which eventually migrated out of Africa and into Europe and Asia. The best-known *Homo erectus*, the Neanderthals, lived in Europe and western Asia between about 200,000 and 35,000 years ago. Neanderthals used stone tools and were among the first people to bury their dead. They were not, however, modern human beings.

Modern humans differed from *Homo erectus* distinctly in physical features, including skulls with high foreheads and tucked-in faces. Furthermore, they made tools of malleable materials such as bone, ivory, and antler as well as stone. The beginnings of modern human culture have been traced to the Palaeolithic era, which lasted to about 10,000 B.C. In that era came human creation of art, religion, control of fertility, technological advances, specialized crafts, and warfare. After 10,000 B.C., they began to domesticate plants and animals and settle in villages that were forerunners of the civilizations that would form around 3000 B.C.

Many scholars call the domestication of plants and animals the "Neolithic Revolution," but change was more evolutionary than revolutionary. After about 7000 B.C., Neolithic agricultural villages were more numerous and made extensive domestic advances. After 3,000 B.C., the

1

Mesopotamian city-states erected a new kind of complex society with social, economic, and class hierarchy. They formed political and religious institutions, invented sophisticated hydraulic systems and other technological advances, created large urban spaces with monumental architectural structures, and used a written language.

The Mesopotamian city-states grew around the valley cut by the Tigris and Euphrates rivers. For all their monumental achievements, they learned the hardships imposed by natural disasters and conquest by surrounding enemies. The Egyptian civilization that grew up in the Nile River valley took shape on the same grand scale as Mesopotamia, but was spared the natural disasters and invasions that scarred Mesopotamian history.

Civilizations also appeared in modern Pakistan and northwest India and in northern China before 2000 B.C. No civilization began in Europe until around 2000 B.C., when the Minoans of Crete, along with their eventual conquerors, created the civilizations that were ancestral to the Greek empire. Mesopotamia and Egypt, though, exerted most influence on many early civilizations, including the Hittites and the peoples of Syria-Palestine.

Multiple-Choice Questions

Choose the best response.

_____ 1. Which species of modern human beings appeared at the earliest about 200,000 years ago and perhaps as recently as 35,000 years ago?
   a. hominids.
   b. Neanderthals.
   c. *Homo sapiens.*
   d. *Homo erectus.*

_____ 2. During which era did the sign of modern human culture begin to appear?
   a. Neolithic
   b. Palaeolithic
   c. Neanderthal
   d. Monolithic

_____ 3. The evolving human activities that led to civilization by 3000 B.C. included
   a. the move by humans from sedentary to mobile existence.
   b. replacement of an agricultural economy by a hunter-gatherer economy.
   c. domestication of animals and cultivation of plants.
   d. forming of the first nation-states.

_____ 4. According to scholars, why did the Mesopotamians invent writing?
   a. As the Mesopotamian economy grew more complex, people needed to take inventories and record transactions.
   b. They found a use for paper, or papyrus, which became a growth industry.
   c. The Sumerians hoped to spread their language to extend their influence and therefore avoid conquest by the Akkadians.
   d. The people of Mesopotamia believed that, to be understood by later generations, they needed a system of written communication.

_____ 5. Hammurabi's Code is significant partly because it
   a. first defined the word *law* in Mesopotamia.
   b. purged the law of retaliation for wounds from the Mesopotamian code.
   c. clearly reveals how idealistic Mesopotamian scholarship and science were.
   d. was more lenient than other documents.

_____ 6. Approximately what percentage of Egypt is habitable by people?
   a. 10 percent
   b. 50 percent
   c. 5 percent
   d. 25 percent

_____ 7. Because of the Nile River's fertilizing floods,
   a. Egyptians were relatively pessimistic compared to other ancient peoples.
   b. the alluvial plain was much friendlier to would-be farmers than were the Tigris and Euphrates rivers.
   c. Egyptian art and literature were focused on the unpredictable universe.
   d. Egyptians had to endure an unstable life that was reflected in their ideology.

_____ 8. According to the authors of your text,
   a. The ancient Egyptian population had a sizable, perhaps predominant, African element and numerous immigrants from Southwest Asia.
   b. Egypt was primarily African and ancient Egyptians were black.
   c. Egypt was a part of the Near East, and therefore ancient Egyptians looked much like modern Europeans.

_____ 9. Which of these was a characteristic of Egypt's Divine Kings?
   a. Egyptians spoke directly "to" the king when addressing him or her.
   b. The Pharaohs were appointed by the gods.
   c. The Pharaohs made "glorious appearances" before their subjects at festivals, jubilees, or celebrations.
   d. The Pharaohs dressed much like their subjects, seeking to feel closer to them.

_____ 10. Which of these was a source of Hittite power?
   a. mastery of the ox.
   b. control of fire.
   c. the rich minerals and farmland in Anatolia.
   d. skill in diplomacy, which kept them at peace with other ancient peoples.

Answers to Multiple-Choice Questions

1. c	3. c	5. d	7. b	9. c
2. b	4. a	6. c	8. a	10. c

Identification

Briefly identify and summarize the historical significance of each of the following:

Ebla

Sargon

Re

Uruk

Ugaritic texts

Neanderthals

Canaanites

Book of the Dead

"Neolithic Revolution"

Hatshepsut

cuneiform

Ramesses II

Ur-Nammu

hominids

Short-Answer and Essay Questions

11. Discuss in detail the human transition from the cave to the town.

12. Analyze the evidence showing how urban life reappeared in Syria around 1400–1200 B.C.

13. What part did Queens and Queen Mothers have in Hittite society?

14. Analyze how the international system collapsed between 1250 and 1150 B.C. and the aftereffects.

15. Mesopotamia and Egypt are considered the world's first two civilizations. Discuss the beginnings of these civilizations and how they influenced the differing early civilizations in the eastern Mediterranean region.

Map Exercise

Map 1.2 Mesopotamia

16. Using your textbook, find the civilizations in the Ancient Near East. Discuss how geography affected the growing civilizations and spreading cultures in the Ancient Near East.

CHAPTER 2

The Book and the Myths: Western Asia and Early Greece

Learning Objectives

After studying this chapter, you should be able to:

1. understand the extreme changes at the eastern end of the Mediterranean Sea during the first half of the first millennium B.C.

2. discuss the stages in the Persian empire's rise to prominence among its neighbors.

3. compare the Assyrian and Persian empires and analyze the greater success and influence of the Persian empire.

4. understand the new conceptions about human life that were formulated in that era.

5. analyze how Hebrew civilization influenced Western historical and religious traditions.

6. discuss in outline the Minoan and Mycenaean civilizations.

Summary

The first half of the first millennium B.C. was a time of great change, moving from bronze to iron for tools and weapons, creating two major empires and one short-lived one, and devising new ideologies about human life and its meaning. Applying iron tools in war was accompanied by more brutal and inhumane warfare. Those methods, along with administrative innovations, led to the vast Assyrian empire in the seventh and eighth centuries B.C. That empire stretched from western Iran to Palestine and, briefly, to Egypt.

The Assyrian empire, known for brutal conquests, skilled warriors, and innovative administrators, reached its apex when invading Egypt in 667 and 664 B.C. Its successor, the Neo-Babylonian empire, along with the Medes, dominated southwest Asia. The Neo-Babylonians are known for their prominent place in the Hebrew Bible, the hanging gardens in Babylon, and their keen interest in astronomy and astrology.

The Phoenicians became world traders, building a civilization that peaked between 1050 and 750 B.C. They spread urbanism to both the European and North African sides of the Mediterranean and served as seafarers, merchants, and slave traders for the region.

The Persian empire reached its height in the first half of the first millennium B.C. At its fullest, the empire reached from central Asia and northwest India in the east to Macedon and Libya in the west. It was a vast, well-organized, and relatively tolerant empire, respectful of its subjects' cultures.

Typical of the era, the Persians organized a new religion, Zoroastrianism. The faith emphasized the triumph of good over evil, redemption by a divine savior, and a system of ethics by which its adherents should live. Like the Persians, the Hebrews or Israelites, founded an ideology to help them explain human life and its meaning. The Israelites moved from polytheism to belief in one god, Yahweh, who was omnipotent. Yahweh gave meaning and purpose to life and history and was merciful and just. The Israelites' belief in Yahweh and the religion they constructed around that belief eventually became Judaism. The Jews produced the first written history, the Old Testament of the Bible.

The Greeks too pondered the meaning of human existence, but focused their beliefs on humanity. Human beings were destined to die and in their belief system their gods did not promise redemption. One must therefore be heroic in life. Greek writers such as Homer glorified heroism and at the same time recognized life's fragility. Homer's writings inspired more questions about human life and its meaning. The Greeks attempted to answer those questions in the middle of the first millennium B.C., profoundly influencing Western culture.

Multiple-Choice Questions

Choose the best response.

_____ 1. The Assyrians were a military power during most of the second millennium B.C. because
   a. they prospered in the silk trade between Mesopotamia and Anatolia.
   b. they were a factor in the balance of power between the Hittites and New Kingdom Egypt.
   c. around 1200 B.C. they conquered Babylonia and expanded their homeland.
   d. they had half a million men with iron weapons.

_____ 2. The Assyrians deported masses of people from conquered countries. Their policy included
   a. deporting entire families.
   b. deporting whole populations.
   c. settling deportees in Israel.
   d. setting up sculptured reliefs and inscriptions to reflect the humane treatment they planned for deportees.

_____ 3. Phoenicians established colonies for several reasons, among them
   a. boosting their lagging population.
   b. serving as a training ground for the Assyrian military.
   c. learning their colonists' language and customs.
   d. finding precious metals.

_____ 4. The Hebrews believed
   a. human achievement is meaningful.
   b. in polytheism.
   c. only the power of the divinity matters.
   d. the one true god had revealed himself to the Assyrians.

_____ 5. The Hebrew Bible consisted of three main sections, including the
   a. Qu'ran.
   b. Torah.
   c. New Testament.
   d. Book of the Dead.

_____ 6. Only about a half-dozen women in the Hebrew Bible serve as leaders of Israel, including
   a. Esau.
   b. Deborah.
   c. Rebecca.
   d. Mary.

_____ 7. Persia succeeded as an empire because the Persians
   a. believed in terrorism and brutality as effective methods in dealing with colonists.
   b. were skilled in administration and organization.
   c. believed it was unnecessary to maintain a large conscript army.
   d. undertook ambitious expeditions that gathered great wealth for the empire.

_____ 8. The religion of ancient Persia, until the Muslim conquest in the seventh century A.D., was
   a. Buddhism.
   b. Christianity.
   c. Zoroastrianism.
   d. Islam.

_____ 9. Europe's first monumental, literate civilization originated at
   a. Crete.
   b. Rome.
   c. Israel.
   d. Mesopotamia.

_____ 10. Homer and Hesiod indicate that in the eighth century B.C., the typical Greek community
   a. was ruled by a flexible group of democratically elected leaders.
   b. was dominated by magi in things that mattered to ordinary people: religion, rendering justice, and providing aid in famine years.
   c. made decisions about war and peace by convening a council of warriors.
   d. had the basic instruments of government that would endure for centuries in Greece: generals, orators, judges, a council, and an assembly.

Answers to Multiple-Choice Questions

1. b	3. d	5. b	7. b	9. a
2. a	4. c	6. b	8. c	10. d

Identification

Briefly identify and summarize the historical significance of each of the following:

Ten Commandments	The Exodus
Alexander the Great	ethical dualism
"Iron Age"	*Iliad* and *Odyssey*
Zarathustra	Israelites
Abraham	Ark of the Covenant
Zoroastrianism	Yahweh
Cyrus the Great	Nebuchadrezzar II

Short-Answer and Essay Questions

11. Compare religious outlooks in the Hebrew Bible and the Homeric poems.

12. Discuss the Phoenicians' role as seafarers, merchants, and slave traders in the world.

13. Analyze how monotheism came about in Hebrew civilization.

14. Discuss the ways in which the Persian king's exaltation countered rebellious tendencies.

15. Agree or disagree, wholly or in part, that the most influential innovations during the first half of the first millennium B.C. were not in commerce, metallurgy, or imperialism but in new ways of understanding human life and its meaning.

Map Exercise

Map 2.1 The Assyrian Empire

16. On the outline map provided, identify Assyria and its neighboring civilizations. Discuss how geography—the hills and coastal plains south of Assyria—affected the number of times the region changed hands during the eighth and seventh centuries B.C.

Map 2.1 The Assyrian Empire

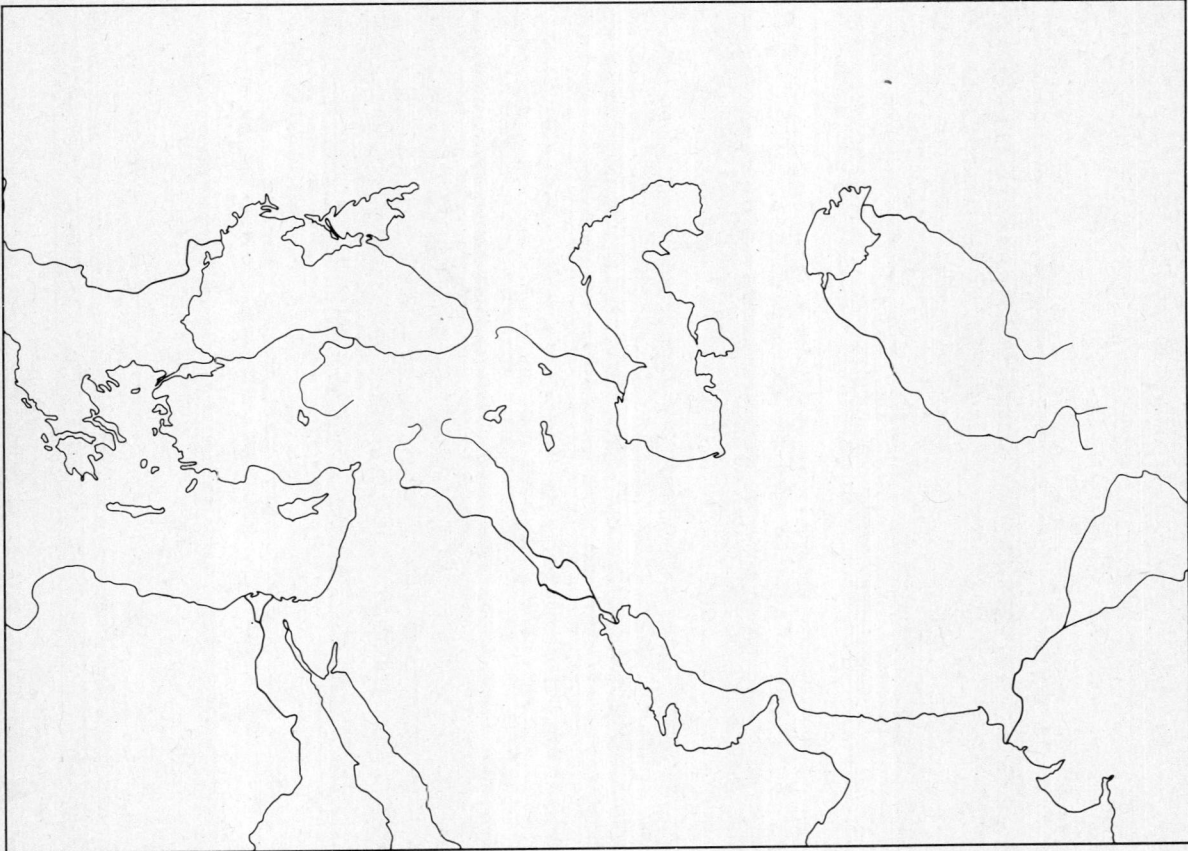

CHAPTER 3

The Age of the Polis: Greece, ca. 750–350 B.C.

Learning Objectives

After studying this chapter, you should be able to:

1. understand the *polis* as an institution in Greek life.
2. trace democracy as it evolved in Greece.
3. discuss how Western philosophy, science, politics, literature, and the arts crystallized in Archaic and Classical Greece.
4. compare Athens with Sparta: history, society, position in the world.
5. discuss the treatment given metics, women, and slaves in democratic Greece.
6. analyze the Greek wars in the fifth and fourth centuries B.C.
7. understand how Socrates and the Sophists affected Greek society.

Summary

Archaic Greece, from about 750 to 350 B.C., was known for assimilating and adapting other cultures as well as for dedication to its own cultural innovations. That was the age of the polis and urban-centered life.

Archaic Greeks lived in small city-states that rarely came together and thus did not create a large empire like those of the Assyrians and Persians. The lack of cooperation between Archaic Greek city-states was obviated by the genius of the polis.

Along with its sometimes tense social cohesion and its military technology, the polis made the Greek city-states unique. The poleis were small, covering the often-tiny urban area and a larger countryside. Each included an acropolis, a defensible hill, an agora or gathering place, and usually one temple. In physical structure the early poleis were unremarkable, but their cultural and political framework thrived because of the hoplite phalanx.

The phalanx symbolized the Archaic Greek competition between politics and war. The tightly ordered units bred *aretê*, or "warrior prowess," which never replaced family loyalty but built a community spirit supporting the poleis.

The Greeks forged democracy but chose not to extend it to women, immigrants, and slaves in their own city-states. Moreover, they constructed an empire that by definition circumvented self-rule by people in the conquered areas.

The paradox of Archaic Greek civilization extended to its religious beliefs. The Greeks created splendid monuments to their deities even as some in their intellectual community decided that the gods served little purpose in their endeavor to understand human existence and the meaning of the universe.

Of the two leading Greek poleis, Athens took pride in its cultural achievements and its dedication to freedom. Sparta, on the other hand, eschewed the intellectual life. Instead, the Spartans lived lives of obedience and austerity in their militaristic city-state.

Athenian government was stagnant in the 460s B.C. Led by Pericles, who came to power in 460 B.C., Athens reached the zenith of its empire. For thirty years Pericles guided Athens and its uniquely talented residents. The city-state augmented its empire and achieved a prosperous economy and cultural greatness. In short, Pericles gave Athens a collective sense of purpose, but it would not last.

Multiple-Choice Questions

Choose the best response.

_____ 1. The Greeks' motives for colonization included
   a. the desire to spread their religion to colonists.
   b. their desire to live up to the Roman name for the Southern Italy and Sicily region, *Magna Graecia* ("Great Greece").
   c. their hunger for land.
   d. their interest in forming communal societies.

_____ 2. The hoplite phalanx was
   a. a tightly ordered unit of heavily armed, pike-bearing infantrymen.
   b. a tightly knit group of democratic leaders in the polis.
   c. a group of slaves who had been captured in battle.
   d. a group of professional soldiers whose service in the military usually lasted nine months each year.

_____ 3. Spartan society was distinctive because of
   a. its openness to outside influence.
   b. its creation with one stroke by the legendary lawgiver Zeus.
   c. its concentrating power in a hereditary, sometimes tyrannical, monarch.
   d. its simple diet.

_____ 4. Between approximately 675 and 500 B.C., the dominant Greek literary form was
   a. drama.
   b. lyric poetry.
   c. comedy.
   d. rhetoric.

_____ 5. The Greek assembly
   a. consisted of 500 executives and 700 public officials.
   b. allowed only great orators, such as Pericles and Demosthenes, to speak.
   c. made decisions about war and peace, friendship and alliance.
   d. consisted of courts, which, with a few exceptions, were open to all citizens, no matter how poor.

_____ 6. The Peloponnesian War (431–404 B.C.)
  a. killed from one-fourth to one-third of the Athenian population.
  b. was won by Sparta and destroyed the Athenian empire.
  c. was undecided for a decade and a half because of Athenian supremacy on land and Spartan mastery of the sea.
  d. demonstrated the Greeks' ability to unite after defeating Persia.

_____ 7. Classical Greek culture was unique for
  a. its introspective poets and alienated figures.
  b. its private individuals who served as major patrons for sculpture and architecture.
  c. its philosophy, with its focus on biology and metaphysics.
  d. its emphasis on the public realm.

_____ 8. The philosopher Plato
  a. wrote dialogues or speeches with more than one speaker rather than straight-forward philosophical treatises.
  b. left a legacy of realism, of which he is one of Western philosophy's greatest advocates.
  c. embraced public life as an Athenian citizen.
  d. had a high opinion of democracy and regularly intervened in Athenian politics.

_____ 9. The greatest Greek writer of comedy in the fifth century B.C. was
  a. Euripides.
  b. Aristophanes.
  c. Aeschylus.
  d. Sophocles.

_____ 10. Though writers of history had preceded Herodotus and Thucydides, the two Greeks are put among the founding historians in the West because of
  a. the unifying themes in their works.
  b. the dogmatic style of their writing.
  c. their emphasis on religion as opposed to war, politics, peoples, and customs.
  d. similarities in their research techniques and writing styles.

Answers to Multiple-Choice Questions

1. c	3. d	5. c	7. d	9. b
2. a	4. b	6. b	8. a	10. a

Identification

Briefly identify and summarize the historical significance of each of the following:

Eupatrids	Cleisthenes
Socrates	Aristotle
Apollo of Delphi	Sappho of Lesbos
Miletus	tyranny
Solon	Pythagoras
Olympic games	oligarchy

Short-Answer and Essay Questions

11. Discuss Spartan society: its foundations and dependence on its army.

12. How did the gods fit into Greek political and social structures?

13. Show how Western philosophy evolved in Greece during the sixth century B.C.

14. Trace the advances in Greek democracy from 508 to 321 B.C.

15. The Greek city-state was unique because of its social cohesion, military technology and formations, and above all, the practice and ideology of citizenship. How influential was the polis as the Greek city-state advanced, and how did it affect citizenship?

Map Exercises

Map 3.2 Phoenician and Greek Colonization

16. On the outline map provided, identify the areas that the Phoenicians settled and identify their main trade routes. In what ways did geography affect the Phoenicians' reputation as master traders and seamen?

Map 3.3 Attica

17. Using your textbook study Athens and its neighboring Greek states. Discuss the Athenian government when ruled by the basileis of the Attic Plain.

Map 3.2 Phoenician and Greek Colonization

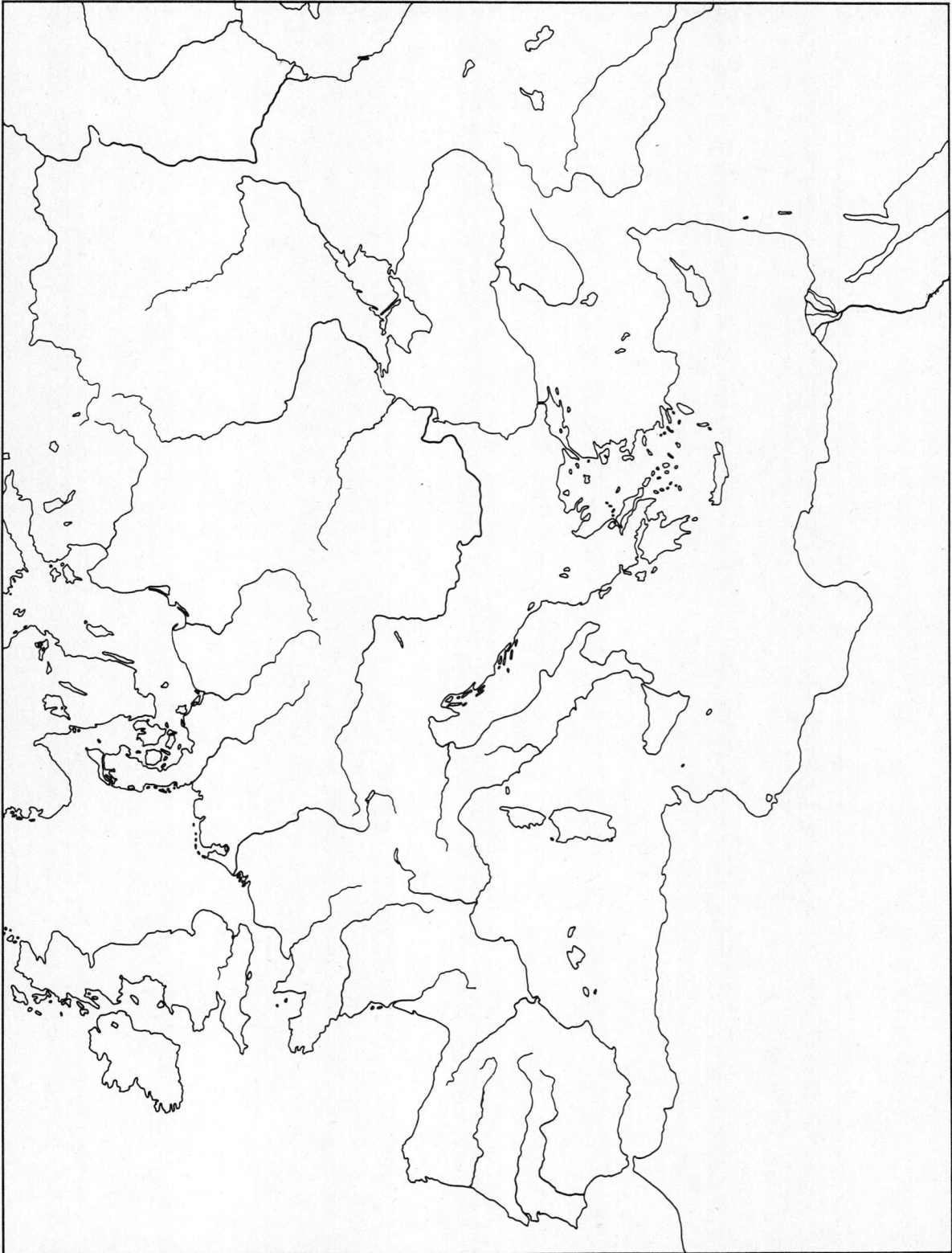

CHAPTER 4

The Hellenistic World

Learning Objectives

After studying this chapter, you should be able to:

1. understand the revolution in the Greek world that brought the Greek city-states to yield power to Macedon.

2. trace the stages in development of the Hellenistic world.

3. analyze how Philip and Alexander changed history in the Hellenistic world.

4. discuss culture in the Hellenistic world.

5. understand the position the federal leagues and kingdoms had in the Hellenistic world.

6. analyze the relationship between Jewish doctrine and Hellenistic religion.

Summary

The Hellenistic world was founded by Philip II of Macedon (382–336 B.C.) and his son Alexander III, later known as Alexander the Great. It took Philip just twenty years to conquer the disunited Greek city-states. He never achieved his goal—absorbing Persia into his empire—but Philip did make himself dominant in Macedon and Macedon dominant in Greece.

Alexander expanded the empire, taking in Egypt and all of western Asia as far as modern Pakistan. He was ruthless, intelligent, talented, charismatic, and cultured. A popular leader, he destroyed whole cultures and peoples in his deadly march toward greater empire, but he also founded no fewer than twenty cities. Ultimately he became a despot. His life's individual achievement was a greatly varied Hellenistic world.

The Hellenistic world of Alexander and his successors included multiethnic kingdoms, ethnically homogeneous city-states, and just about everything else between those extremes. Its government was a monarchy that dabbled in republicanism and experimented with federalism and social revolution.

Though the Hellenistic kingdoms and city-states lived with each other in almost constant low-level tension, Isocrates successfully promoted the idea of Pan-Hellenism in some areas. Generally, however, Greeks and Macedons retained their identity as imperial masters; the Egyptians, Syrians, and Persians, held theirs as conquered colonists.

The federal leagues and kingdoms came to dominate the Hellenistic world as the polis diminished. The citizen-warrior ideal was questioned, along with the whole point of political activity. The antihero replaced the hero in the hearts and minds of Hellenistic peoples, and some, particularly women, who had been tangential in the Archaic Greek world gained relatively freer status.

Jews also enhanced their standings in the Hellenistic world. Their doctrines about ethics and the interior dialogue between God and humanity appealed to the Greeks. The Jewish rituals had less appeal for them. Still, a god-savior with whom one could have a close relationship and who would guarantee comfort, peace, and eternal life after death captured Greeks' attention. When traditional culture was in decline, therefore, religion held interest for Hellenistic peoples. Hellenism and Judaism drew closer and eventually joined in a new religion: Christianity.

Multiple-Choice Questions

Choose the best response.

_____ 1. As a border state, Macedon was distinguished by its
   a. efficiently organized polis.
   b. citizens' relatively genteel lifestyles.
   c. rich resources and manpower.
   d. inept leader, Philip.

_____ 2. During his last seven years, Alexander the Conqueror
   a. practiced a novel policy: fusing Greek and Persian cultures, a sharp break from the traditional Greek ethnocentrism.
   b. engaged in a limited number of strategic military campaigns designed to secure the Macedonian empire in India.
   c. became a more benevolent ruler because his power was secure.
   d. was preoccupied by his place in history and wrote his memoirs to set the record straight.

_____ 3. The main sources of enslavement in the Hellenistic world included
   a. heredity and indebtedness.
   b. uprisings by tenant farmers.
   c. war and piracy.
   d. plantation, household, and administrative workers.

_____ 4. The wealthiest, most sophisticated, and most durable Hellenistic kingdom was
   a. Antigony.
   b. Aetolia.
   c. Achaea.
   d. Ptolemaic Egypt.

_____ 5. The "New Comedy" in the Hellenistic world
   a. was raucous and ribald.
   b. focused on domestic and private matters.
   c. focused on public matters like war and politics.
   d. symbolized a return to Aristophanes' style.

_____ 6. The most popular of several competing philosophical schools in the Hellenistic world was:
   a. Stoicism.
   b. Epicureanism.
   c. Cynicism.
   d. Skepticism.

_____ 7. The traditional Greek religion with Olympian gods came under attack in the Hellenistic era because
   a. the popularity of the polis rose and that of the Olympian gods declined.
   b. Hellenistic philosophers believed that all traditional Greek gods except Zeus were primitive, unsophisticated, and immoral.
   c. the Greeks considered some gods embodiments of cities, but after Alexander's conquests, the Olympians shared the spotlight with deified kings such as Alexander.
   d. Hellenistic scholars, who were not popular with the people, espoused the gods' virtues in their writings.

_____ 8. During the struggle over Hellenism, Judaism took in new and lasting elements, including
   a. a literature calling for spiritual resistance to the foreigner.
   b. a monolithic religion from the various Jewish sects.
   c. the end of anti-Semitic literature in the ancient world.
   d. easing tension between the large Jewish minority and the Greek majority in Alexandria.

_____ 9. The Jewish sect that proposed a kind of democratization of Judaism, emphasizing study and prayer in small groups known as "gatherings" or "houses of learning," was the
   a. Essenes.
   b. Sadducees.
   c. Gentiles.
   d. Pharisees.

_____ 10. The greatest cultural innovation in the Hellenistic age was
   a. that the female nude became as popular a subject for sculptors as the male nude.
   b. the retreat from values associated with the citizen-warrior ideal in the Classical city-state.
   c. the antihero, often a man whose success depended on a woman's kindness and love.
   d. freer movement, property rights, and public participation by women.

Answers to Multiple-Choice Questions

1. c	3. c	5. b	7. c	9. d
2. a	4. d	6. a	8. a	10. b

Identification

Briefly identify and summarize the historical significance of each of the following:

Aratus of Sicyon   Isocrates
Seleucids   The Museum
Darius III   Menander
Asoka   Euclid
Antigonus Gonatus   Federal Leagues

Short-Answer and Essay Questions

11. Discuss in detail how large and varied the Hellenistic kingdoms were.

12. Compare Hellenistic Athenian literature with Classical literature.

13. Analyze the Hellenistic advances in science and medicine.

14. Analyze how Greek and Jewish cultures mixed in the Hellenistic world.

15. Agree or disagree, wholly or in part: "The fourth century B.C. brought the greatest revolution to the Greek world since the rise of the polis four hundred years earlier."

Map Exercises

Map 4.1 Conquests of Philip and Alexander

16. On the outline map provided, identify Alexander's eastern campaign route. Discuss how Alexander's eastward campaign affected his soldiers and his empire.

Map 4.2 Hellenistic Kingdoms, Leagues, and City-States

17. On the outline map provided, identify the areas in Asia and Africa controlled by Alexander's successors and discuss the Greeks' immigration policy toward residents in these areas.

Map 4.1 Conquests of Philip and Alexander

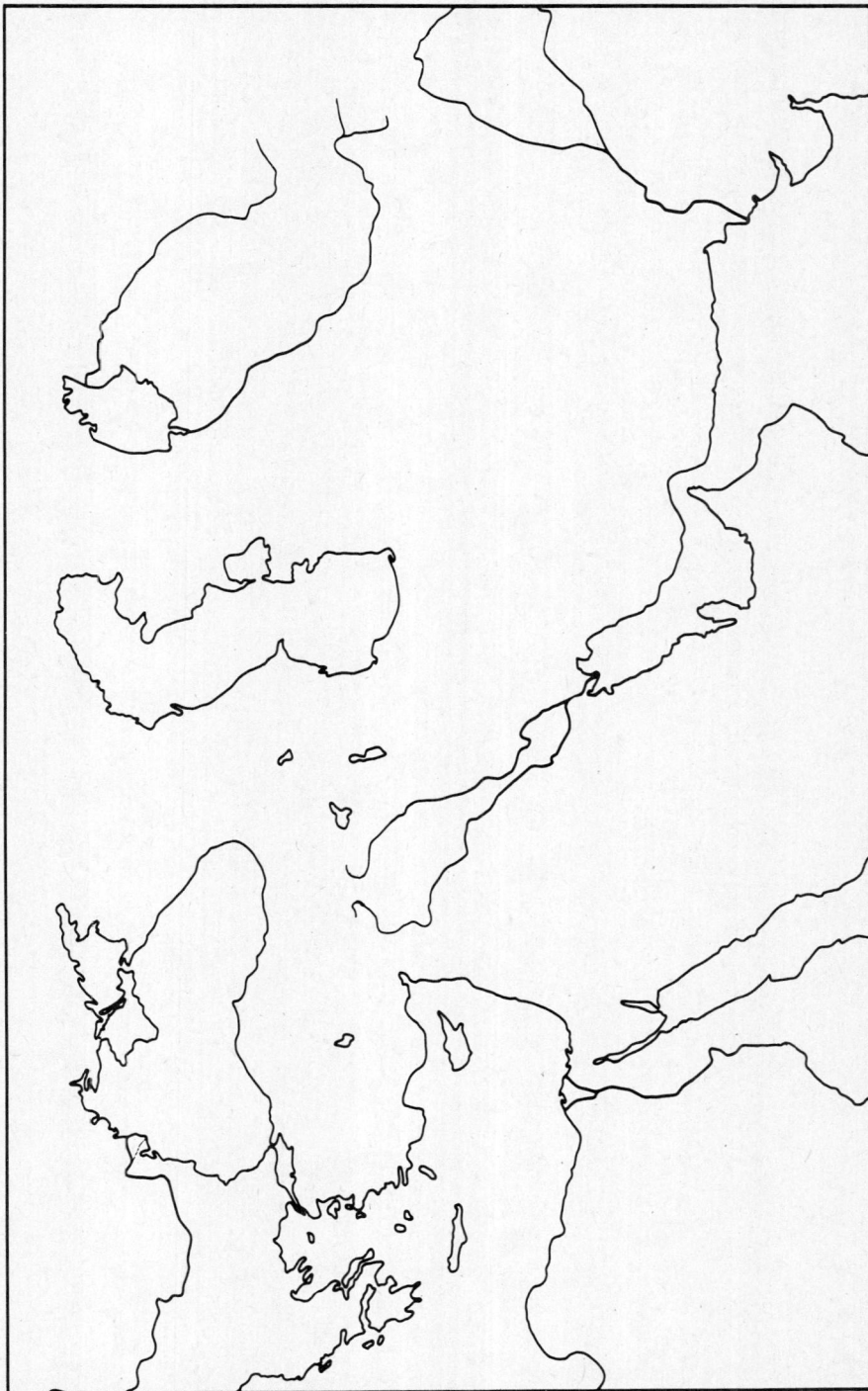

Map 4.2 Hellenistic Kingdoms, Leagues, and City-States

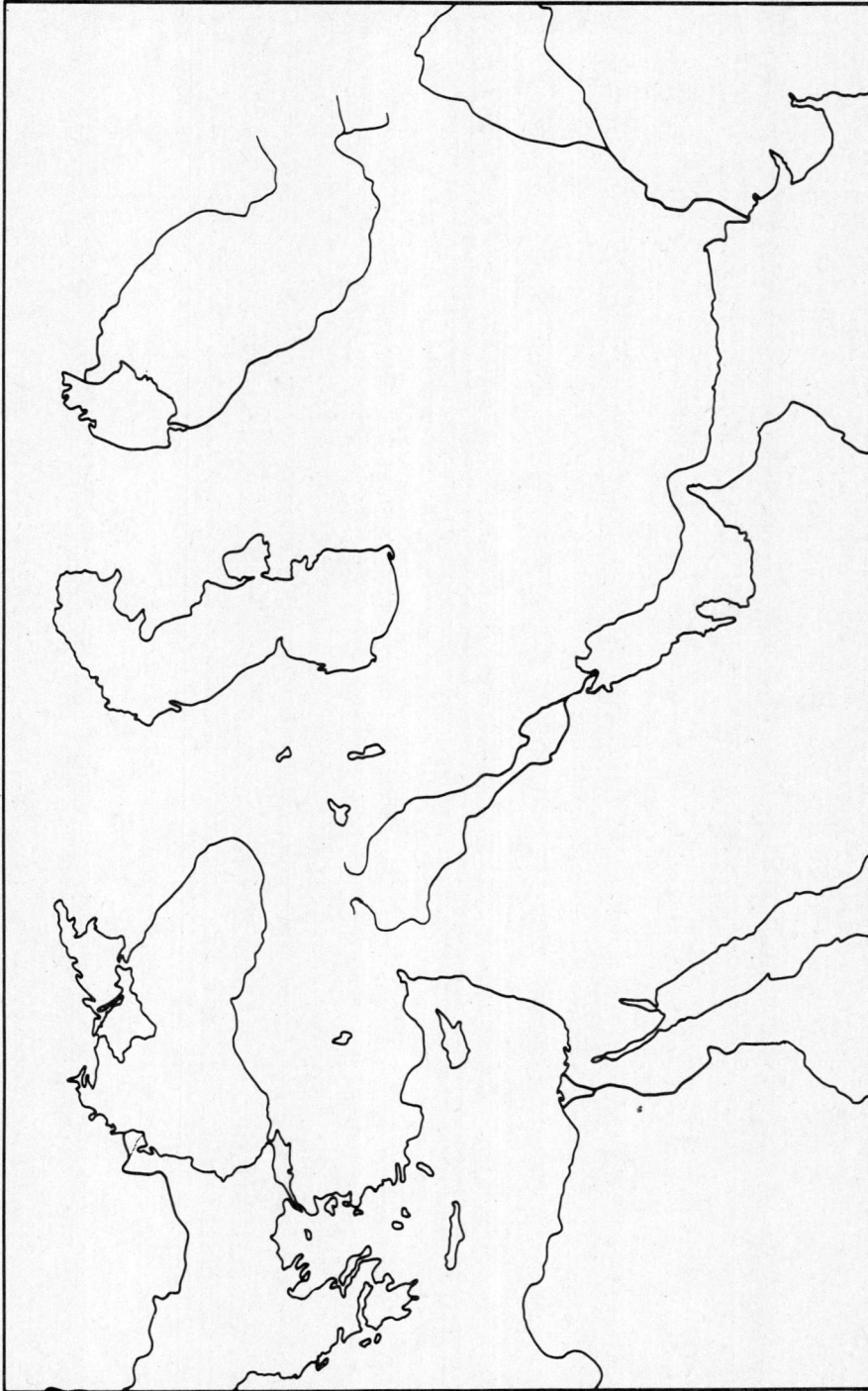

CHAPTER 5

The Rise of the Roman Republic

Learning Objectives

After studying this chapter, you should be able to:

1. discuss the world of early Italy.

2. understand how the Roman Republic was founded.

3. analyze the government and society in the Early and Middle Republic.

4. explain how Rome expanded from an Italian city-state to a world empire.

5. analyze the relationship between Rome and its Empire.

Summary

In the second century B.C., the Roman world successfully combined republican government with imperialism and Greek culture to form a stable and yet flexible society. The Republic's oligarchy accommodated the aristocracy and the newly rich, with competitive instincts similar to those of the Archaic and Hellenistic Greeks, and the people's land hunger. It created a government more open to the plebeians' leaders and with room for popular representation. Amid these changes, the traditional social hierarchy retained its form, protecting political stability.

The Roman Republic utilized its flexibility beyond its political institutions by wisely consolidating central Italy into the fold and then treating the peoples of central Italy with mixed firmness and generosity. Rome extended citizenship to colonists, promoting loyalty to the Republic and giving them a stake in its success.

Beyond central Italy, the Roman Republic was interested in creating an empire that would ensure its safety and security. These fears, ambitions, and greed led Rome to conquer the remainder of the Mediterranean region.

Rome's flexibility extended to absorbing its colonists' culture, particularly that of the Greeks. Romans had little of their own literature until the second century, but recognized and understood the greatness of others' works. The Romans exhibited their own cultural power in ambitious roadbuilding and shipbuilding programs, both contributing to the Republic's success in imperialism.

But the Republic's success ultimately led to its downfall. By the mid-second century B.C., Rome had physically ensured its safety from outside forces. Struggles within the Republic caused problems in the Late Republic. From the Greeks the Romans gained culture but loosened previous restraints. The military campaigns that gained physical security for Rome had been accomplished by conscripting the peasants, leaving a weakened peasantry. The influx of slaves from military conquests made plantation farming profitable, but the elite, greedy for land, confiscated it from those weaker than they. The hierarchy that had produced stability for the growing Republic was creating a growing social instability that endangered the later Republic.

Multiple-Choice Questions

Choose the best response.

_____ 1. The greatest influence on early Rome was that of the
   a. Villanovans.
   b. Greeks.
   c. Etruscans.
   d. Samnites.

_____ 2. The legal head of a Roman family was
   a. always the father of the nuclear family.
   b. the oldest living male ancestor.
   c. always the mother of the nuclear family.
   d. a council of the senior male relatives of the family

_____ 3. The earliest Roman religion focused on
   a. the spirits and powers in inanimate forces.
   b. the Greeks' Olympian gods.
   c. one omnipotent god.
   d. a number of gods related to the cult of Lucretia.

_____ 4. As the Roman Republic's government evolved, it exhibited
   a. inefficiency and indifference.
   b. inability to send men to serve as commanders or governors away from home.
   c. refusal to create and use symbols of power.
   d. adaptability.

_____ 5. In the Early Republic the plebs consisted of
   a. the mass of poor peasants.
   b. the mass of poor peasants and a few wealthy men who were not patricians.
   c. 136 wealthy families.
   d. the mass of poor peasants, a few wealthy men who were not patricians, and 136 wealthy families.

_____ 6. The factors motivating Rome's early conquests were
   a. lust for conquest and hatred for outsiders.
   b. self-control and shrewdness.
   c. greed, particularly land hunger.
   d. personal ambitions of a warrior elite and the conflict prevalent in early Italy.

_____ 7. Rome's extraordinary military success has been attributed to.
   a. organizational ability and love of order.
   b. an ideology that thrived on chaos and instilled reverence for civil disobedience.
   c. an egalitarian, noncompetitive environment for Roman generals.
   d. ruthless treatment of allies.

_____ 8. As a result of the Punic Wars
   a. Carthage enlarged its empire to absorb Spain and Asia Minor.
   b. Rome conquered Greece and Asia Minor.
   c. wealthy Romans became less wealthy and more inhibited.
   d. life for the peasants of Italy was easier because of better treatment by the wealthy.

_____ 9. In the last two centuries B.C., Roman rural society transformed from
   a. independent farming to farming heavily dependent on slave labor.
   b. *latifundia* to subsistence farming.
   c. independent farming to former farmers making their living from trade.
   d. *latifundia* to agriculture that contributed less to elite wealth.

_____ 10. In the traditional education of a Roman aristocrat before the second century B.C.,
   a. Greek slaves were acquired by wealthy families to educate their sons in Greek language and literature.
   b. parents and close family friends were the primary influence.
   c. Greek freedmen set up schools offering instruction in Greek language and literature.
   d. sons were sent to Latin grammar schools.

Answers to Multiple-Choice Questions

1. c	3. a	5. b	7. a	9. a
2. b	4. d	6. d	8. b	10. b

Identification

Briefly identify and summarize the historical significance of each of the following:

Latin League	Romulus
Sibyl	*nexum*
Marcus Porcius Cato	Appian Way
Lucretius	*curiae*
Hannibal	Carthage
Titus Maccius Plautus	Publius Cornelius Scipio

Short-Answer and Essay Questions

11. Discuss the ways in which Rome built connections between the East and the West.

12. Analyze how Etruscan culture affected early Rome.

13. Discuss the paterfamilias as the focus of power in Roman households.

14. Analyze the reciprocal relationship between patrons and clients in Roman society.

15. Republican government, successful imperialism, and absorption of Greek culture are the three outstanding trends in Roman society in the second century B.C. In what ways did these qualities contribute to the rise and ultimate fall of the Roman Empire?

Map Exercises

Map 5.1 Early Italy and Region of City of Rome

16. Using your textbook study Rome, Latium, and the Tiber River. In what ways did location in Latium give Rome a strategically potent position in the Italian peninsula?

17. Note the Roman Empire under Augustus and the territory added by the time of Hadrian. In what ways did the Roman Empire's expansion contribute to its decline?

Roman Revolution and Imperial Rome, 133 B.C.–A.D. 284

Learning Objectives

After studying this chapter, you should be able to:

1. understand the revolution from the Gracchi to Caesar.
2. analyze Augustus and the Principate.
3. discuss the Roman peace and its collapse in the third century.
4. analyze Christianity's origins and explain why it expanded and underwent persecution.
5. understand the mystery religions in Late Antiquity.

Summary

Between the second century B.C. and the second century A.D., Rome became an ever more stratified society. The ruthlessly ambitious Commodus ruled tyrannically and was assassinated in 192, ending Roman peace. Roman rulers grew more militaristic. Between 235 and 284, Rome had more than twenty emperors, many of whom seized power with the help of legions or guardsmen who had assassinated those they had earlier helped assume the throne.

Moreover, the safety so desired by the Early Republic proved elusive. Rome faced problems in the east from the Persians and from the Germanic tribes along the Rhine–Danube border and in Britain, the Dacians, and the Balkans.

Roman safety was also challenged from within its borders. The social stresses that had begun in the Late Republic intensified. Peasants fighting with the Roman army lost their farms. The elite refused to share its wealth and prosperity. The peasantry sought revenge by supporting patrons who raised armies to win land for their followers and *virtu* for themselves. In the colonies, the flexibility of Roman imperialism gave way to greed, bureaucracy, and taxation. By the first century B.C., the Republic had collapsed under its own problems.

Octavian created a new empire and declared himself Augustus, the first emperor. Under Augustus's leadership, the new Republic enjoyed two centuries of renewed stability. He stabilized the frontiers, shared power with the elite, provided farms for all veterans, raised colonists to equal Italians' status, and guaranteed peace by controlling most of the armies himself.

The *pax Romana*, at its height between A.D. 96 and 180, was an era of enlightened emperors, thriving cities, and intellectual vitality. Peace nourished literature and architecture in the empire and helped promote stability. Rome became a multicultural empire of 50 million or more inhabitants engaging in a dynamic dialogue that advanced the empire's cultural life. An era of spirituality enabled an obscure sect in southwest Asia to slowly spread its doctrine, Christianity, around the Mediterranean and into northern Europe.

Multiple-Choice Questions

Choose the best response.

_____ 1. The Late Republic in Rome was an age of
    a. idealism.
    b. individualism.
    c. communal spirit.
    d. internal peace.

_____ 2. Tiberius Sempronius Gracchus's land-reform law
    a. allowed wealthy landowners to purchase up to 160 acres of public land.
    b. required former landowners to pay for improvements, such as buildings or plantings, on their property prior to passage of the law.
    c. was applauded by many senators who felt Tiberius filled the necessary role of super-patron to Roman citizens.
    d. set up a commission to repossess excess land and redistribute it to the poor.

_____ 3. Julius Caesar sponsored many reforms, including
    a. conferring Roman citizenship liberally.
    b. decreasing the Senate from 900 to 600 members.
    c. introducing the Gregorian calendar to the Western world.
    d. halting public building programs in Rome.

_____ 4. The assassination of Julius Caesar led to
    a. an end to civil war in the Republic.
    b. years of renewed order in the Empire.
    c. democracy and election of a more benevolent ruler.
    d. belief among the Liberators that the assassination was justified by the public interest.

_____ 5. Rome's legal system
    a. adapted flexibly to changing circumstances.
    b. suffered because the disenfranchised in the Late Republic sought unreasonable goals.
    c. outlawed the notion of the legal expert who devoted himself to explaining and interpreting the law.
    d. was complex and intricate and therefore needed interpretation.

_____ 6. The Augustan period
    a. was one of cruelty, decadence, and excess.
    b. was one of affluence, especially in Italy.
    c. was one of hunger, driving peasants into the hands of ambitious generals.
    d. marked the end of rural poverty and slavery in Italy.

_____ 7. The so-called Five Good Emperors included
    a. Caligula.
    b. Nero.
    c. Julius Caesar.
    d. Marcus Aurelius.

_____ 8. The third-century Roman Empire experienced
    a. stability heretofore unseen in the empire.
    b. centralization of the Roman elite.
    c. an ever-widening spiral of crisis.
    d. transfer of power, during the reign of Septimius Severus, from the army to the senate.

_____ 9. The popularity of Christianity and other new religions in the early Empire indicates both Roman successes and failures, including
    a. civil unrest caused by the Roman elite, which helped spread new ideas.
    b. the elite's blend of traditional state and family religion as well as emperor worship and Stoic philosophy, which failed to satisfy ordinary people's spiritual needs.
    c. centralized Roman rule, which allowed movements to grow among marginal populations.
    d. acceptance and understanding for Judaism in the empire.

_____ 10. The Gnostics
    a. were an amalgam of Christian, Jewish, and pagan ideas.
    b. were the least prominent nonorthodox group of Christians circa A.D. 80 to 150.
    c. embraced the material world.
    d. were moderate in asceticism or license

Answers to Multiple-Choice Questions

1. b	3. a	5. d	7. d	9. b
2. d	4. d	6. b	8. c	10. a

Identification

Briefly identify and summarize the historical significance of each of the following:

Jesus of Nazareth
pax Romana
Pontius Pilate
Virgil
Lucius Cornelius Sulla Felix
Livia

Marius
Cleopatra
Julio-Claudians
Cicero
Augustus
Paul of Tarsus

Short-Answer and Essay Questions

11. Discuss in detail Cicero's contributions to the Late Republic.

12. Compare Virgil's and Horace's works.

13. Analyze the culture of Roman peace.

14. Discuss how the Sermon on the Mount typified Jesus of Nazareth's teachings.

15. Analyze Augustus's reforms. Did he lay the foundations for the prosperous two centuries of the Roman peace, or did he hasten Rome's decline?

Map Exercises

Map 6.1 The Roman Empire in the Late Republic

16. On the outline map provided, identify the area held by the Roman Republic. In what ways did the wars with Numibia and in North Africa and Gaul weaken the republic?

Map 6.2 The Roman World in the Early Empire

17. On the outline map provided, identify the site of the naval battle of Actium and the surrounding areas. How did Octavian lay the foundations for the prosperous two centuries of Roman peace after his forces defeated Anthony and Cleopatra in 31 B.C?

Map 6.3 The Expansion of Christianity to A.D. 600

18. On the outline map provided, identify St. Paul's routes as he spread Christianity. How did geography help spread the religion? How did it hold up Christianity's spread? (Note: The outline map differs from the map in the main text.)

Map 6.1 The Roman Empire in the Late Republic

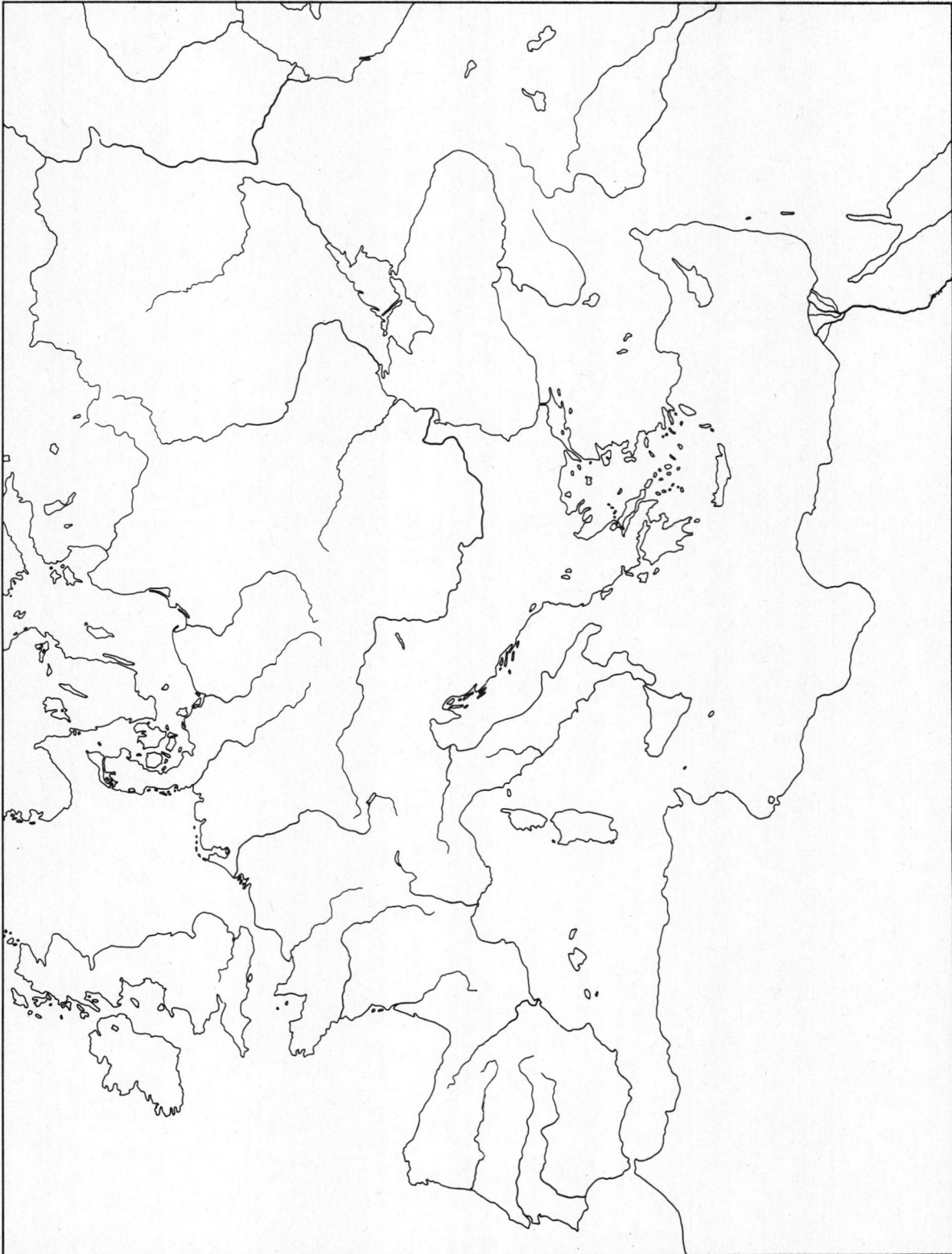

Map 6.2 The Roman World in the Early Empire

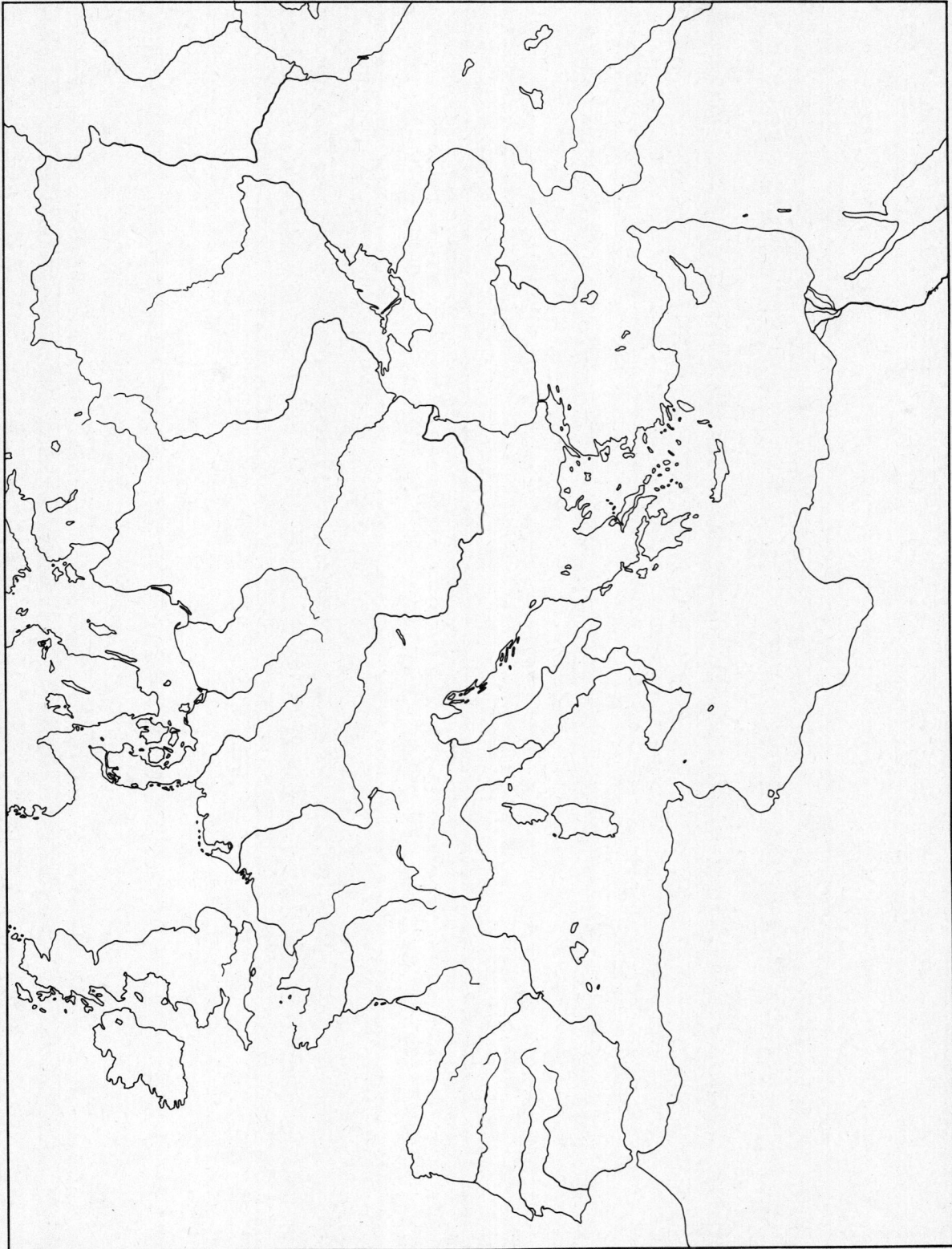

Map 6.3 The Expansion of Christianity to A.D. 600

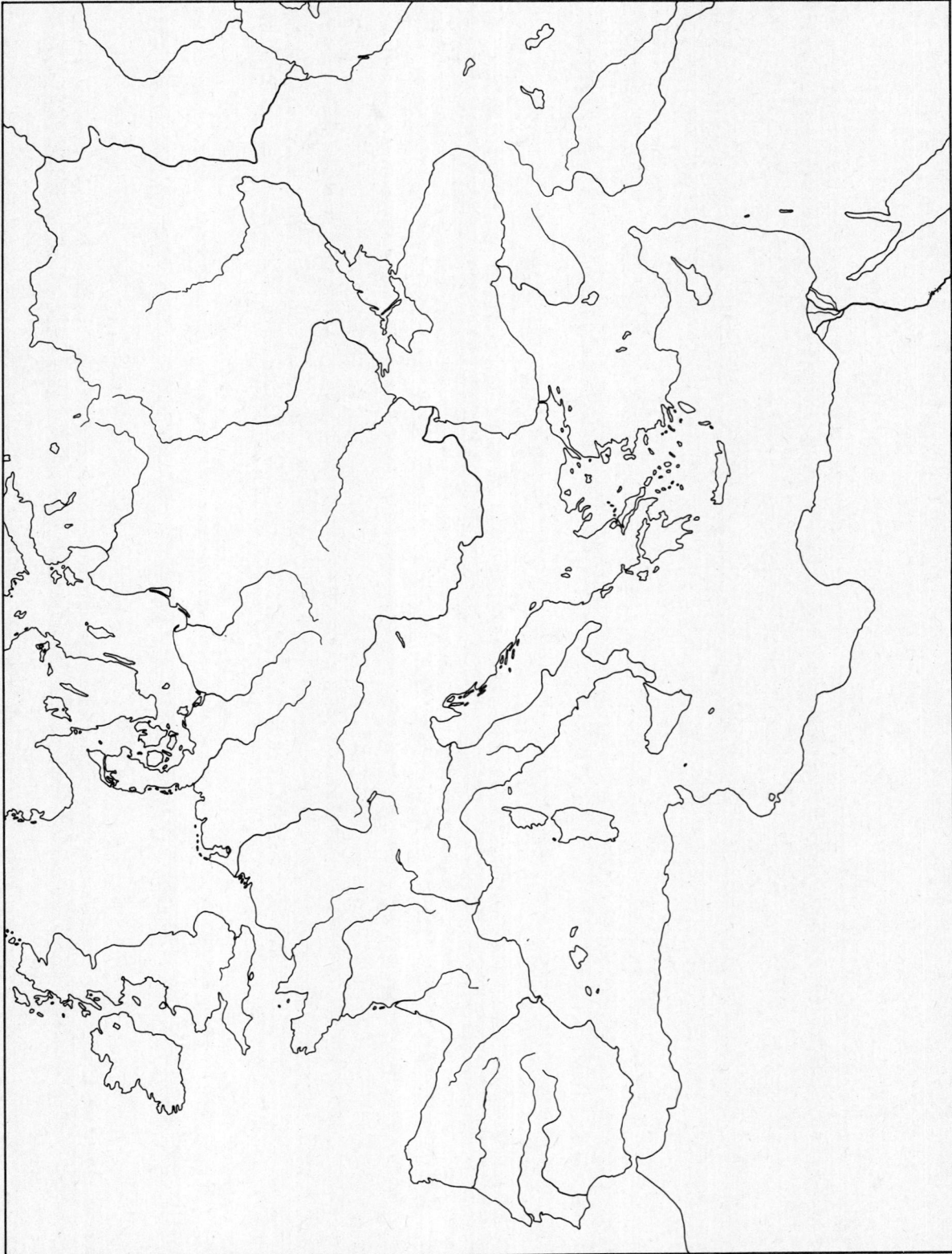

CHAPTER 7

The World of Late Antiquity, ca. 300–600

Learning Objectives

After studying this chapter, you should be able to:

1. understand how the Roman world responded to the crisis in the third century.
2. discuss the militarization of the government.
3. analyze why the people of Late Antiquity rejected classical culture.
4. understand the continuation of the formal aspects of classical culture that were continued by Christian writers.
5. summarize social structure in Late Antiquity.
6. discuss the paradox of the nearly invisible boundary between change and continuity in Late Antiquity.

Summary

Late Antiquity, from about 300 to 600, is an era of transformation amid continuity. Rome responded to the third-century crises, including political assassination, civil war, and threatened frontiers. Peace had been elusive. The Empire had seemingly grown too large for one ruler.

Diocletian (284–305) temporarily checked the chaos in the third century. He chose as his administrators the most talented men he could find and created a larger, decentralized bureaucracy to officiate over Rome's newly reorganized smaller provinces. Diocletian split the Empire into four imperial capitals to further decentralize the Empire and make it more manageable. He enlarged the army to meet the Empire's defense needs, enlisting Germans to help defend the borders. Diocletian's peace did not last. When he resigned in 305, the decentralization of the Empire into four regions disintegrated. Civil wars and dynastic inheritance made a comeback.

In 324, Constantine became sole ruler of the Roman Empire. He followed the general policies of Diocletian, ruled autocratically, and consulted his most trusted advisers. Under his rule Byzantium was founded, laying the groundwork for the eventual split in the Empire between East and West.

Amid this change continuity held the Empire together. Most Romans remained poor farmers. The social hierarchy remained the same, the same types of people retaining power and wealth. In Late Antiquity, however, these people were likely to be kings and bishops. It was a triumph for Christianity as an institution to become part of the traditional hierarchy.

Christianity offered social principles and a coherent system of thought. Christians had begun the era as a persecuted minority. By 600 they held, with Jews, the distinction of being the only officially authorized faiths in the Roman world.

Multiple-Choice Questions

Choose the best response.

_____ 1. Diocletian believed an ideological flaw in the Roman imperial system was that ever since the Principate, emperors
    a. pretended to be lineal descendants of the Republican magistrates, but their real power was based on the military.
    b. failed to effectively use their military power to extend the Empire's borders.
    c. had adopted eastern, especially Persian habits, such as wearing a jeweled diadem and rarely appearing in public.
    d. had expanded the imperial administration by doubling the number of officials and dividing the old, large provinces into smaller ones rather than adding new territories.

_____ 2. Diocletian's reforms
    a. were applauded by a small but influential group of 2,000.
    b. added to the senatorial order of military and civic responsibility.
    c. were sensible but costly.
    d. allowed senators to acquire enormous wealth, powerful offices, and personal prestige, and thus local influence.

_____ 3. Constantine's military policies
    a. included moving experienced troops from the frontiers, which actually reduced border attacks.
    b. created divided loyalties and conflicts of interest by recruiting Germans into the field armies and leaving frontier defenses to German auxiliaries.
    c. ended the period of Roman militarization, during which the Empire had become a vast armed camp.
    d. freed the Empire's financial resources from maintaining a military establishment that was expensive, socially diverse, and politically volatile.

_____ 4. Diocletian has been remembered for his treatment of Christians because he
    a. undertook the last persecution of Christianity.
    b. embraced Christianity, believing that the presence of Christians in his army boosted morale.
    c. saw Christians as a positive force in his desire to promote unity.
    d. opened numerous churches and supervised the first widespread distribution of the Scriptures.

_____ 5. Constantine dealt with religious controversies by
   a. persecuting those who disrupted unity in the Empire.
   b. embracing the pagan state cults and holding priestly offices in several of those cults.
   c. summoning theologians to guide him and by assembling church councils to debate issues and promulgate solutions.
   d. embracing Arianism.

_____ 6. After the Edict of Milan, the church
   a. attracted a clear majority of the Empire's population.
   b. struggled to survive, because it had offended the Empire's leaders.
   c. saw a significant decline in membership.
   d. saw an increase in the Christian clergy's prominence everywhere except in Rome.

_____ 7. Christians believed that
   a. birth, wealth, and status helped a person's chances for salvation from sin.
   b. hierarchies had no place in the basic offices of the church.
   c. the structure of the church should be different from the flawed structure of the secular world.
   d. a "democracy of sin" within the church made all Christians equal in God's eyes.

_____ 8. Rome was sacked in 410 by the
   a. Ostrogoths.
   b. Franks.
   c. Visigoths.
   d. Lombards.

_____ 9. In Late Antiquity, education was confined to the elite and consisted of Latin or Greek grammar, dialectic, and
   a. Bible studies.
   b. rhetoric.
   c. history.
   d. Roman, Egyptian, and German cultural studies.

_____ 10. By the 530s, the Western Roman Empire
   a. had disappeared.
   b. was flourishing.
   c. was witnessing the beginning of the Germanic invasions.
   d. had benefited from years when Rome's best leaders resided in and worried mainly about the West.

Answers to Multiple-Choice Questions

1. a	3. b	5. c	7. d	9. b
2. c	4. a	6. a	8. c	10. a

Identification

Briefly identify and summarize the historical significance of each of the following:

Diocletian	Benedict of Nursia
Edict of Milan	Theodosius I
Constantine	*Life of Anthony*
The City of God	Valentinian
Attila	Justinian
Julian	Clovis

Short-Answer and Essay Questions

11. Discuss the effect of the decision in 363 to appoint two rulers for the Roman Empire.

12. From the time of Augustus, the Roman regime had attempted to promote unity. How did they do so? Why were their attempts ultimately futile?

13. Analyze the shifting social hierarchies in Late Antiquity.

14. How successfully did the Western Roman Empire incorporate the German peoples?

15. Agree or disagree, wholly or partially: "The paradox of Late Antiquity is the nearly invisible boundary between change and continuity."

Map Exercises

Map 7.1 Diocletian's Division of the Roman Empire

16. On the outline map provided, identify the four regions and rulers in Diocletian's division of the Roman Empire. Was it necessary to divide the administration of the Empire?

Map 7.3 The Germanic Kingdoms in the Sixth Century

17. On the outline map provided, identify the Germanic kingdoms in the sixth century. How did the Germans' arrival change the Roman Empire?

Map 7.1 Diocletian's Division of the Roman Empire

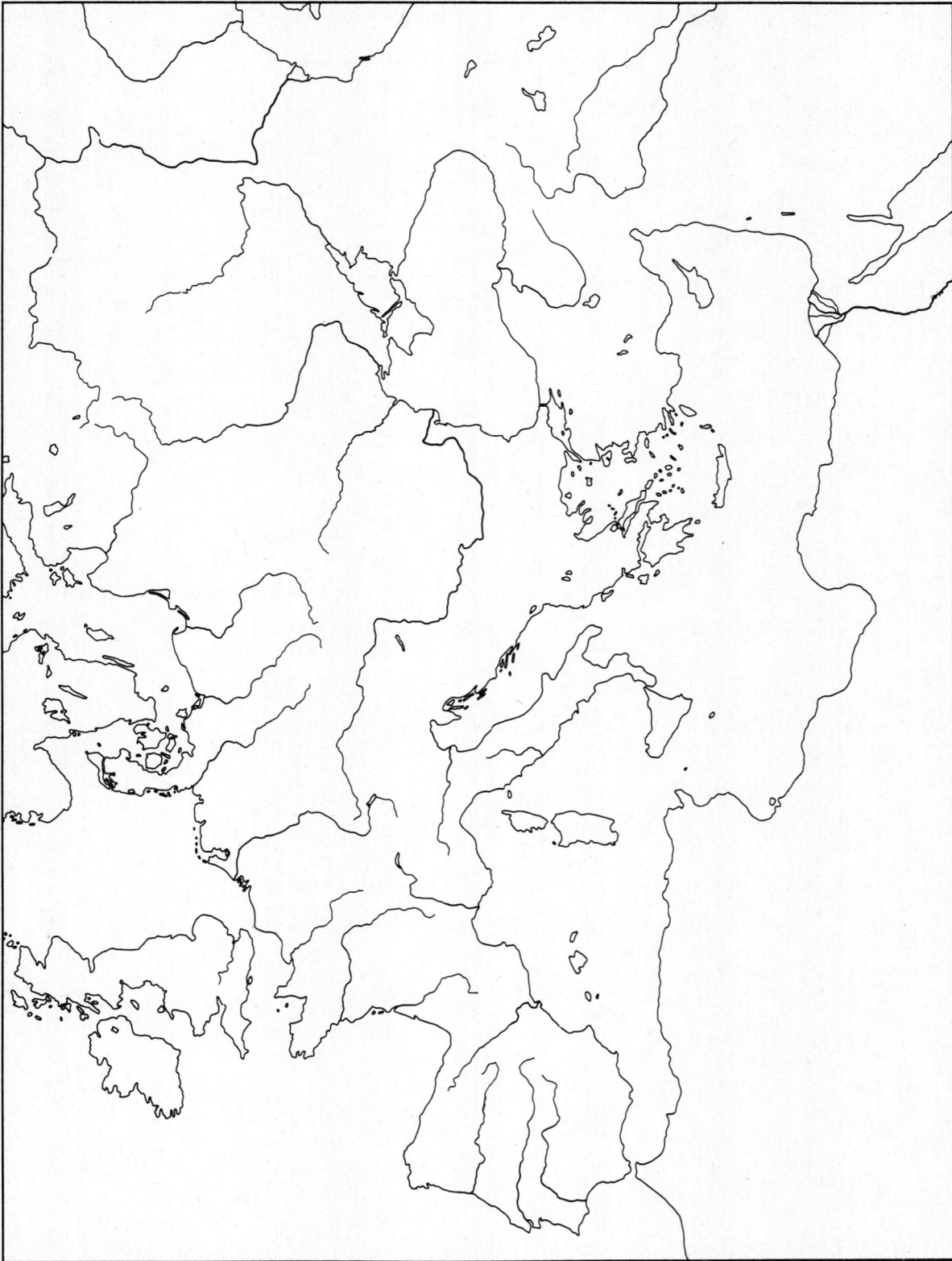

Map 7.3 The Germanic Kingdoms in the Sixth Century

CHAPTER 8

Early Medieval Civilizations, ca. 600–900

Learning Objectives

After studying this chapter, you should be able to:

1. understand the rapid change in the seventh century, the consolidation and reform in the eighth century, and the renewed challenges in the ninth century.

2. analyze the political and social structures of the Islamic, Byzantine, and Frankish worlds.

3. how successful was each of the empires in maintaining its world?

4. understand Islam's rise and expansion.

Summary

In the Early Middle Ages remarkable similarity appeared in the developing Islamic, Byzantine, and Latin worlds. In the seventh century each of these societies experienced rapid, dynamic change. During the eighth century each consolidated and reformed its empire. In the ninth century the Islamic, Byzantine, and Latin worlds experienced renewed challenges.

The three empires had similarities in their political, religious, and ideological makeup. The Islamic, Byzantine, and Latin worlds created political states with centralized governments, ruled by powerful leaders who, they believed, had been chosen by God to lead them. In all three empires, the central governments administered outlying areas. All described their governments' mission as religious—for Islam, Orthodox Catholicism, or Roman Catholicism, respectively. These religions also provided social cohesion within the societies they served and defined and inspired their cultural lives.

Two of the three empires were different at the end of the Early Medieval era than they had been at the beginning. Between 750 and 1000, Carolingian rulers united the Frankish kingdoms and dominated Western life. They created a loosely organized though adequate government and an effective army. The Islamic world had, by military conquest, created an empire by 750 extending from the Indus River in the east to Spain in the west. Furthermore, the Umayyad caliphs in Damascus founded a dynamic new culture by supporting the arts and education. By the end of the ninth century, however, the Islamic and Frankish empires had broken down into smaller units. The empires had been pulled apart by leadership by varying calibers, unpredictable foreign attacks, and the diverse population.

The Byzantine Empire, on the other hand, maintained its traditions and thus its strength and confidence through the Early Middle Ages. Justinian I streamlined the government, codified the law, and promoted artistic and intellectual pursuits. His efforts to reconquer the West and establish religious unity were not so successful. Still, the Byzantine Empire was smaller than the Roman Empire had been and managed to preserve its state even in the face of danger. Its ultimate decline was slow, its conquest by the Ottoman Turks almost six centuries in the future.

Multiple-Choice Questions

Choose the best response.

_____ 1. Muslims believed
   a. that their responsibilities within the *umma muslima* were confined to themselves and their clan.
   b. that Allah was the most powerful of the Roman gods and worked in harmony with the less-powerful dieties to control the world.
   c. that because of the hegira experience, Islam was a religion of exile, of total separation from the ordinary world, and of total dependence on God.
   d. in the Nicene Creed, which maintained that Christ was "one in being with the Father."

_____ 2. The pillars of Islam sustained a faith that
   a. stressed a simple, uncompromising belief and practices affirming that belief and building a sense of community.
   b. asked followers to pray at specified times each week with their heads facing Medina.
   c. produced an elaborate theology, intricate doctrines, and permanent creed.
   d. was led by a hierarchic clergy.

_____ 3. The conversion of the Visigoths to Christianity
   a. allowed the Germans to extend their empire, knowing they would be forgiven for any sins committed if they later repented.
   b. ended the career of Archbishop Isidore of Seville, who had approved the missionary activity that led to the conversion, against the wishes of the secular leaders of the Roman Empire.
   c. permitted close cooperation between the church and the monarchy and placed the human and material resources of the church at the disposal of the crown.
   d. led to civil war by the end of the seventh century, as Goths and Hispano-Romans in Visigothic Spain fought to secure their culture's predominance in the region.

_____ 4. The most effective of the early Germanic kingdoms was created by
   a. Bede.
   b. Einhard.
   c. Attila.
   d. Clovis.

EARLY MEDIEVAL CIVILIZATIONS | 49

_____ 5. To accomplish their goals the Carolingians
    a. sought alliances with the enemies of the Franks to restore the region's territorial integrity.
    b. fought with leaders of the church, both episcopal and monastic, for the right to convert central Germany and expand Frankish influence.
    c. allowed Arabs to raid parts of Gaul, provided that they shared the booty from these raids with the Franks.
    d. formed alliances with powerful noble families in many regions.

_____ 6. Carolingian art had
    a. decorated manuscripts that showed awe of the past.
    b. innovative work that prominently displayed animal and geometric decorative motifs from Irish and Anglo-Saxon art.
    c. an informality that was a break from the composition of classical art.
    d. originality, in that artists did not use the mysteries of Christian theology as their subject.

_____ 7. The Carolingian empire did not outlive the ninth century because
    a. it failed to grow beyond the border of Bavaria.
    b. the Carolingians made no effort to build a unified culture.
    c. the empire included many small regions, each with its own resident elites, linguistic traditions, and traditional cultures.
    d. the Carolingians attempted to rule the empire with one emperor but without local rulers.

_____ 8. The Treaty of Verdun
    a. divided the Carolingian Empire into three realms.
    b. gave France and Germany their final shape.
    c. managed to unify the empire from several smaller states.
    d. prevented further attacks on the Franks by Arabs, Magyars, and Vikings.

_____ 9. In 632, the Meccan elite chose as _caliph_, or "successor to the prophet" Muhammad,
    a. Umar
    b. Uthman
    c. Mu'awiya
    d. Abu Bakr

_____ 10. Factors that contributed to the Byzantine Empire's stability included
    a. the weakness of the Islamic Empire.
    b. the sophisticated and effective Byzantine bureaucracy.
    c. its strict separation of church and state.
    d. its alliance with Western Europe.

Answers to Multiple-Choice Questions

1. c	3. c	5. d	7. c	9. d
2. a	4. d	6. b	8. a	10. b

Identification

Briefly identify and summarize the historical significance of each of the following:

Heraclius   Medina
Leo III   Abbassid Revolution
Muhammad   Carolingian Renaissance
Constantinople   Bedouins
Bede   Pope Gregory I
Qur'an   Charlemagne
hegira   Irene

Short-Answer and Essay Questions

11. Discuss the Arab world before Muhammad.

12. Analyze the Islamic civilization's rise to world power.

13. Examine the eighth-century recovery of the Byzantine Empire under guidance by Leo III and his successors. Why did the dynasty begin to unravel at the end of the century?

14. Discuss how a papal state was created in Italy in the eighth century.

15. Analyze why the Byzantine Empire managed to defend its territory through the tenth century when the Islamic and Frankish worlds could not do so.

Map Exercises

Map 8.2 The Byzantine Empire in the Eighth and Ninth Centuries

16. On the outline map provided, identify the territorial boundaries of the Byzantine Empire and Constantinople. How was the empire able to transform its military, institutional, and cultural structures to create a regime that lasted until 1204?

Map 8.3 The Carolingian World

17. On the outline map provided, identify the area over which Charlemagne exerted direct or indirect control. How and why was this area divided, ultimately forming France and Germany?

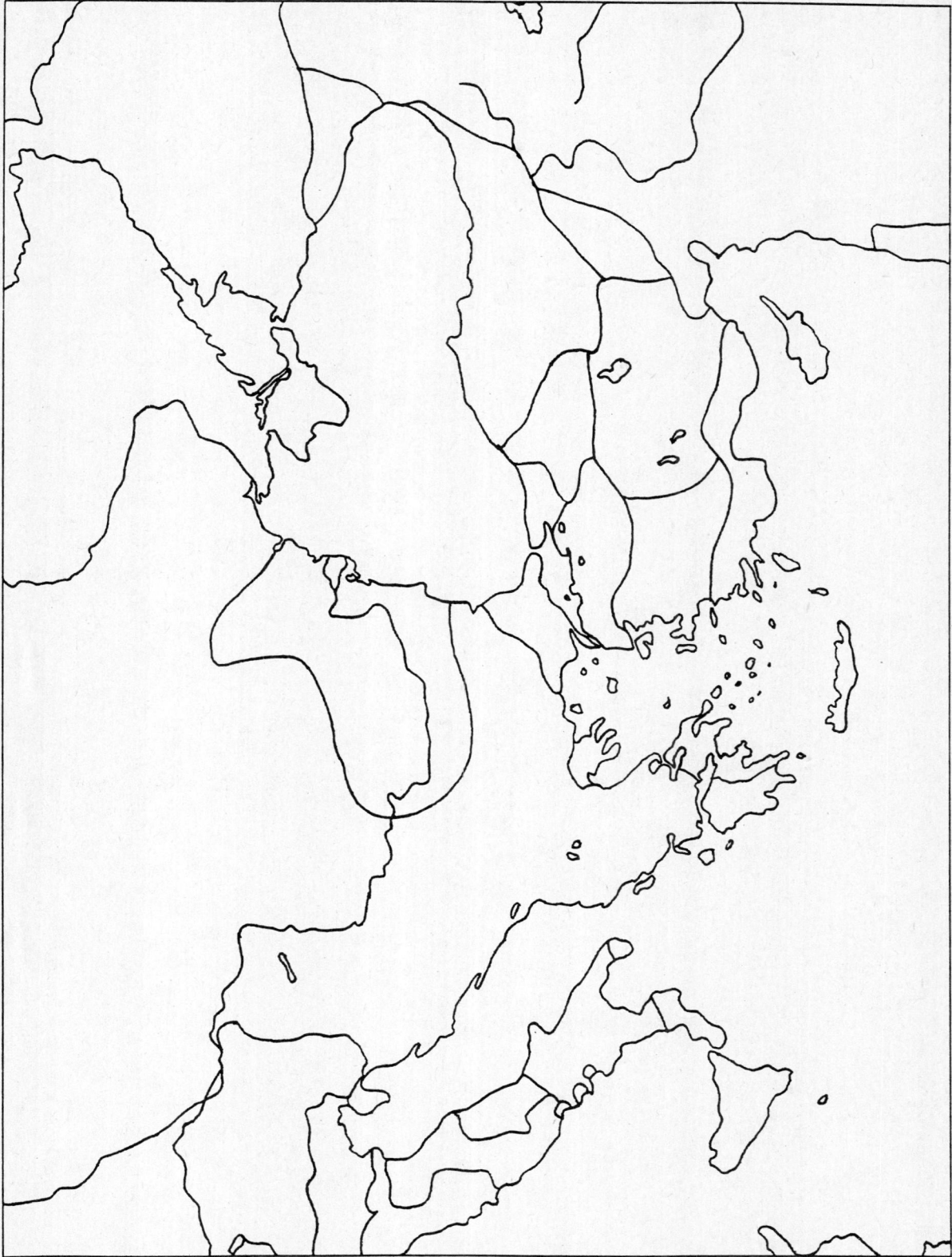

Map 8.2 The Byzantine Empire in the Eighth and Ninth Centuries

Map 8.3 The Carolingian World

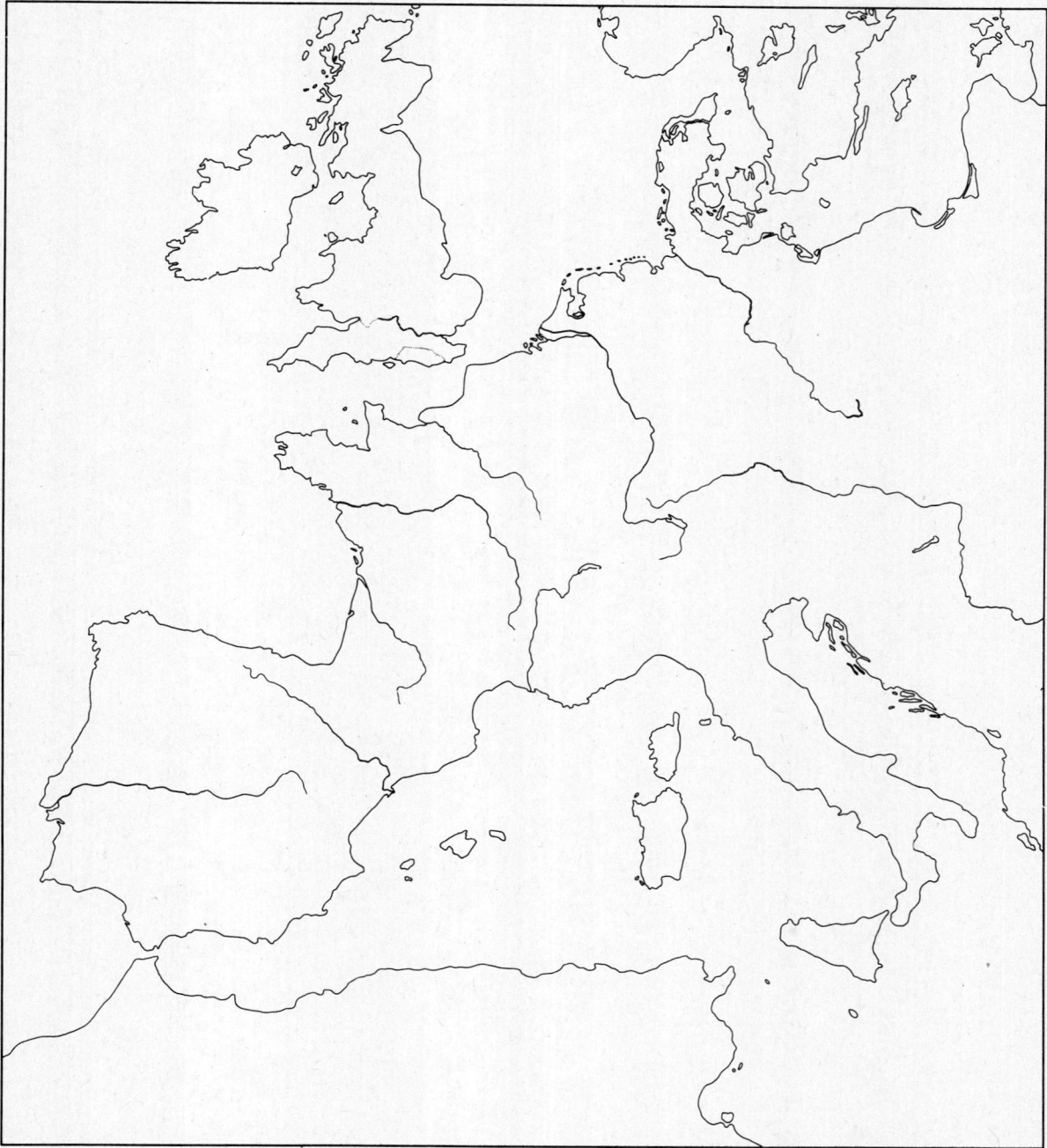

CHAPTER 9

The Frontiers of the Latin West, ca. 600–1300

Learning Objectives

After studying this chapter, you should be able to:

1. understand the size and complexity of the West, including England, Europe, the Celtic lands, Scandinavia, the Slavic countries, Byzantium, and Islam.

2. discuss relations among the parts of the West.

3. explain how the frontier regions in the West developed.

4. discuss the beginnings of the Celtic, Scandinavian, and Slavic states, political systems, Christian churches, social structures, and economies.

5. explain how the Islamic states and the Byzantine Empire changed and became more or less part of the West.

6. summarize cultural change in each of the aforementioned regions.

Summary

For all their differences, frontiers in the Latin West circa 600 to 1300 exhibited undeniable similarities. The frontier of Latin Europe consisted of the Celtic lands, Scandinavia, the Slavic world, Byzantium, and the Islamic world. Each region had a central government that was increasingly bureaucratic as it battled inhabitants over issues of local interest. Populations increased across the board as did economic prosperity, except in Russia and parts of the Islamic world. Social hierarchies formed as nuclear families replaced large kin groupings as the basis for social organization. Only in some Byzantine and Islamic places did kinship groups hold some social ground. Religion helped create and cement social bonds and unity and support the frontiers' secular institutions. At times in the diverse Slavic and Islamic worlds, religion was divisive. In each area, vernacular culture evolved alongside learned languages. Ultimately the peoples who lived on the frontiers enjoyed long, complex relationships with the Latin West. They provided manpower for armies, goods for trade, recurrent elements for thematic art, and characters for literature. In short, they made major contributions to the developing West.

The Celtic lands, Scandinavia, and the Slavic lands became part of the West between 900 and 1300. The Byzantine Empire began the slow decline that led to its downfall in 1453. Russia survived invasion by the Mongols and the Islamic world. The Islamic empire had served as a conduit carrying Greco-Roman cultures to later generations. From the tenth century on, it concentrated on the East and on the divisions within its own world.

Thanks to the land of the Western frontier, the West became both more and less than it had been in the Roman Empire and the Hellenistic world. The frontiers were complex societies, influenced by the West and, in turn, influencing development of the West.

Multiple-Choice Questions

Choose the best response.

_____ 1. The first man to rule most of Wales was
    a. Brian Boru.
    b. Rhodri the Great.
    c. Howell the Good.
    d. Kenneth MacAlpin.

_____ 2. After the Norman Conquest,
    a. kings of England sometimes desired to extend their authority into the surrounding Celtic lands.
    b. kings of England sometimes created independent Norman power blocs beyond the Celtic frontier.
    c. "Normans," as these descendants of Vikings were called, settled in the West Frankish realm known as Normandy.
    d. Normans immediately began crossing the border into South Wales.

_____ 3. Women in Celtic societies
    a. could inherit land and by law could act independently.
    b. could not be divorced by their husbands.
    c. were able, if they had talent and ambition and were part of the aristocracy, to join convents.
    d. shared status ranks with their menfolk but derived little power or privilege from them.

_____ 4. Most Celts earned a living by
    a. becoming artisans.
    b. engaging in agriculture.
    c. becoming merchants.
    d. working for the city government in such places as Dublin, Limerick, and Waterford.

_____ 5. The Scandinavian area that had more land and a better climate than any other was
    a. Norway.
    b. Sweden.
    c. Finland.
    d. Denmark.

_____ 6. Twelfth-century Byzantium had widespread economic advancement, demonstrated by
    a. steadily decreasing population and agricultural production.
    b. increased trade, with more money in circulation.
    c. decaying urban life.
    d. prosperity that was equitably distributed.

_____ 7. Three forces critical to the beginnings of state building in Scandinavia included
   a. greater power and wealth gained by some men or families in specific areas.
   b. the influence of the Roman Catholic Church.
   c. the development in the eighth century of hierarchies of officialdom, territorial instead of personal rule, court ceremonials, and official documents.
   d. originating the ordered routines of complex societies.

_____ 8. From early in the ninth century the most advanced Christian commercial power in the western Mediterranean was
   a. Genoa.
   b. Rome.
   c. Venice.
   d. Constantinople.

_____ 9. Several features exemplify the history of all Slavic peoples and regions, including
   a. very complex relations with surrounding peoples.
   b. little regional or ethnic diversity.
   c. the presence almost everywhere of stable, large-scale political entities.
   d. a shared sense of themselves as one people.

_____ 10. In the eleventh century, Muslim political thinkers identified three components of the caliphal office, including
   a. succession to the prophet by primogeniture.
   b. directing the believers' worldly affairs.
   c. custody of the finances.
   d. enforcing obligatory military service.

Answers to Multiple-Choice Questions

1. c	3. d	5. d	7. a	9. a
2. a	4. b	6. b	8. c	10. d

Identification

Briefly identify and summarize the historical significance of each of the following:

Ibn Sina	Hesychast Movement
St. Patrick	O'Neill
Norman Conquest	Prince Grufydd ap Cynan
Book of Kells	Slavs
Cyril and Methodius	Edward I
Robert Bruce	Jinghiz Khan
Cnut	Anna Komnena

Short-Answer and Essay Questions

11. Trace the development of the early Celtic kingdoms.

12. Compare the Western, Southern, and Eastern Slavs.

13. Discuss themes that you notice in the historical development of the Scandinavian lands.

14. Analyze how the Islamic state decentralized between the tenth and thirteenth centuries.

15. Agree or disagree, wholly or in part, with the textbook authors' statement: "Between the ninth and thirteenth centuries, 'The West' became both more and less than the Roman Empire and the Hellenistic World."

Map Exercises

16. Using your textbook, study the political and historical boundaries of the Slavic kingdoms. How did geography influence the divisions of Slavic peoples?

Map 9.5 The Islamic World at the End of the Abbasid Caliphate, 1258

17. On the outline map provided, identify the Islamic world and its main divisions. In what ways did religion unify the Islamic world? In what ways was it divisive?

Map 9.5 The Islamic World at the End of the Abbasid Caliphate, 1258

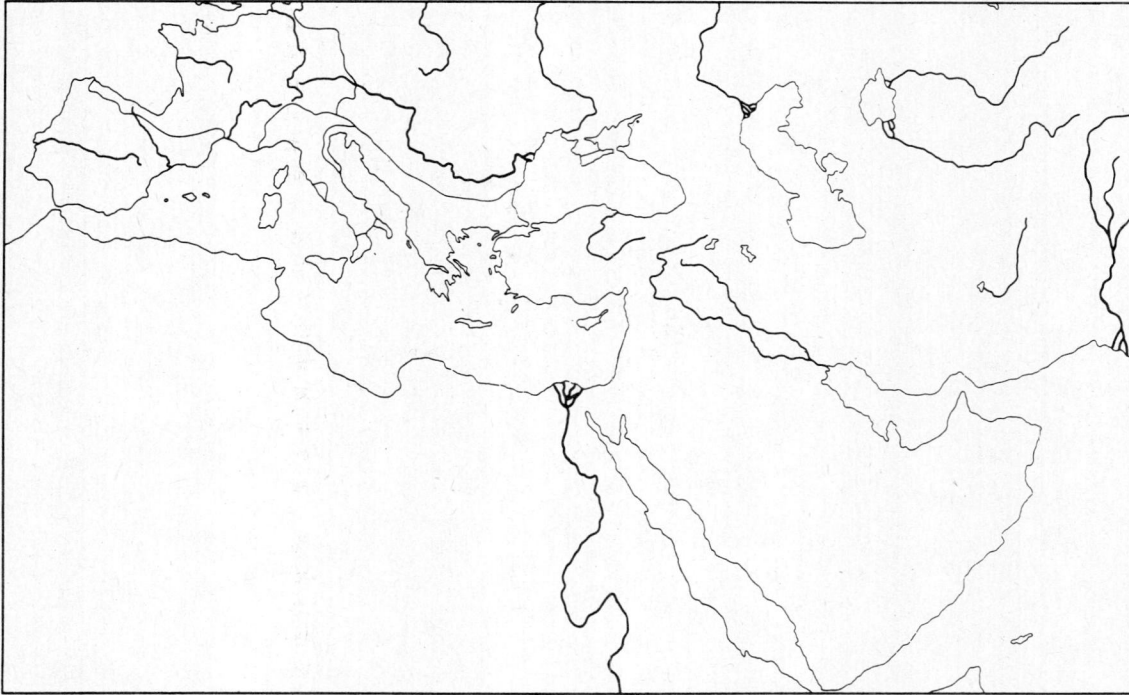

The Expansion of Europe, ca. 900–1150

Learning Objectives

After studying this chapter, you should be able to:

1. understand the signs of expansion in Europe around 900 to 1150.

2. discuss the traditional order in European society.

3. understand the elements of unification in Germany and the German Empire.

4. summarize the rise of Capetian France and Anglo-Saxon England, the Norman Conquest, and the progress of the Reconquista in Spain and Italy.

5. outline cultural life in the Age of Expansion.

6. discuss the First Crusade.

Summary

The twelfth century brought growth in population, prosperity, confidence, and territory to Europe. Centralizing monarchies appeared in England, France, Spain, and Germany and locally, stable and creative communities were numerous.

The population of Europe had begun its slow rise during the Carolingian era, from about 30 million in 1000 to 55 million in 1200. This rise is credited to larger families; though infant mortality was still a common part of life, no significant plagues were around, new land was being brought into agricultural production, and new technologies were being applied.

New technology in agriculture, transportation, mining, and manufacturing brought prosperity, confidence, and interdependence. As fields yielded a return on seed at eight or ten to one, the surplus was used to feed the growing European urban centers.

While agriculture and technology changed, the traditional order of agricultural European society was solidifying. The nobility, the clergy, and the peasants continued in their often reciprocal roles in society even as rural society was taking on a decisive new shape. Left out of the tripartite order were townspeople, ever more active in European life, and non-Christians. Towns had their own hierarchy, though it was relatively ill-defined and inflexible compared to the traditional order.

The church had an important part in twelfth-century European life. It experienced several waves of reform activity. Monastic reformers attempted to positively influence the education, morals, and spiritual lives of religious communities. But reformers also created problems when they challenged the rulers' right to interfere in ecclesiastical affairs. Writers of the Latin letters and vernacular literature thrived and complemented each other's works.

Europeans aggressively sought to expand their influence. The Normans conquered England and southern Italy, Germans expanded into Slavic Europe, and Spanish Christians pushed back Muslims in the Iberian peninsula. Most famous of the moves toward European expansion was the First Crusade to "liberate" the Holy Land from the Turks. It was to be the first of twelve Crusades and the only one deemed successful.

Multiple-Choice Questions

Choose the best response.

_____ 1. The average family size in Europe in the twelfth century was
  a. 3.5.
  b. 5 to 6.
  c. 6 to 7.
  d. 7 to 8.

_____ 2. The three-field system of crop rotation
  a. allowed estates to cultivate 75 percent more than had been possible.
  b. allowed two-thirds of the land to be in constant use.
  c. resulted in diminished flexibility for farmers.
  d. eased out the system of alternating winter crops, spring crops, and fallowing.

_____ 3. The most highly prized chivalric virtue was
  a. military prowess.
  b. loyalty.
  c. open-handed generosity.
  d. honor (reputation).

_____ 4. Cluniac monks
  a. toiled long hours at manual labor.
  b. greatly emphasized liturgical prayer.
  c. spent relatively few hours in solemn devotion.
  d. promoted the idea that the church was to be deeply involved in the world.

_____ 5. Though the structure of individual manors varied tremendously across Europe, some trends were fairly consistent, including
  a. dues owed by peasants.
  b. increased labor services.
  c. lords' tendency to split peasants' payment into cash and kind.
  d. reorganization of the days per year of work for peasants on the lord's domain.

_____ 6. The tripartite model of social organization in Europe left out two groups of people, including
  a. peasants and lords.
  b. clergy and peasants.
  c. lords and non-Christians.
  d. non-Christians and townspeople.

_____ 7. The major factor in the growth of towns was
        a. rise in productivity and profitability of medieval agriculture.
        b. decline in productivity and profitability of medieval agriculture.
        c. increased local exchange.
        d. relentless growth of a money economy.

_____ 8. Though unimpressive as an individual, Louis VI contributed a great deal to twelfth-century France, including
        a. shifting the focus from the monarchy's grandeur to its power.
        b. reducing the circulation of coins.
        c. promoting St. Denis as a patron saint for France, with a shrine in Paris.
        d. holding smaller, more intimate assemblies than any since the Carolingian era.

_____ 9. The period from the tenth century to the twelfth is especially important in Italian history because
        a. the Spanish involved themselves in the affairs of Italy, Rome, and the papacy.
        b. bands of Viking adventurers began a conquest of southern Italy and Sicily.
        c. in northern and central Italy in the eleventh century a distinctive type of urban institution, the commune, began to appear.
        d. Pope Nicholas II defeated the Norman leader Robert Guiscard.

_____ 10. The First Crusade was perfectly consonant with the ethos of the knights of western Europe because
        a. for some years churchmen had been advancing the ideal of men who eschewed knighthood for a life fighting God's enemies and aiding His people.
        b. the vernacular literature of the age glorified the idea of liberating Jerusalem from the Turks.
        c. the Peace of God movement, outlawing, among other things, fighting near churches, had finally been disbanded.
        d. knights were born and trained to fight.

Answers to Multiple-Choice Questions

1. c	3. a	5. c	7. a	9. c
2. b	4. b	6. d	8. c	10. d

Identification

Briefly identify and summarize the historical significance of each of the following:

Alfonso I	Gorze
Gregory VII	Concordat of Worms
feudal system	Rodrigo Díaz de Vivar
Urban II	Cistercians
Templars and Hospitallers	*Beowulf*
Otto I	

Short-Answer and Essay Questions

11. Discuss the conditions that contributed to growth in the population of Europe between 1000 and 1200.

12. Analyze the relationship among the three orders of European society in the eleventh and twelfth centuries.

13. Discuss the role of noble women in the chivalric world.

14. In what ways were the tenth and eleventh centuries a decisive period in reshaping rural society?

15. Analyze the two sides in the "Investiture" controversy.

Map Exercise

16. Find the three fronts along which the Reconquista proceeded, as described in the text. Explain the campaign's goal and its success or failure.

CHAPTER 11

Medieval Civilization at Its Height, ca. 1150–1300

Learning Objectives

After studying this chapter, you should be able to:

1. understand the relationship between the Holy Roman Empire and the papacy.

2. discuss how central governments evolved in France, England, Spain, and Italy.

3. outline economic life in twelfth-century Europe.

4. summarize social and religious movements in twelfth-century Europe.

5. outline the later Crusades.

6. describe twelfth-century medieval culture at its zenith.

7. analyze the last medieval crisis in which church confronted state.

Summary

European economy in the mid-twelfth and thirteenth centuries continued to prosper. In Germany, Frederick Barbarossa ascended to the throne in 1152, beginning a decisive chapter in German history. In the next century, the Holy Roman Empire would first recover from its twelfth-century problems and then collapse. Like Germany, France showed great promise. Unlike Germany, France fulfilled that promise. France produced a strong government under Louise VII, who built on the foundations laid by his predecessors. Even Louis was faced with a vassal, Henry, who controlled more land than he did. France ended the century with a new French saint, Joan of Arc, and was the cultural leader of Europe. The reign of Philip IV brought the medieval French monarchy to the apex of its power. England too showed promise. When Henry II ascended the throne he began reforms that restored efficiency and made England Europe's best-governed twelfth-century state. He also made it clear that he intended to hold onto and control his land on the European continent, causing friction between England and France. King John's behavior prompted English barons to force John to sign the Magna Carta in 1215, committing English kings to get baronial consent before levying new taxes, to administer justice according to established procedures, and to recognize subjects' rights. Edward I completed the development of royal institutions begun by Henry by, among other things, establishing Parliament.

At the beginning of the thirteenth century, Pope Innocent III ruled over a church whose power often exceeded that of European monarchs. By the end of the century, Boniface VIII issued the bull *Clericis laicos*, which forbade taxing the clergy without papal permission. Edward I complied; Philip IV did not. Instead he fought the measure by using antipapal propaganda and an embargo on exporting gold bullion, coin, and valuables to Rome. Boniface relented, and in 1297 issued the bull *Esti de statu*, which allowed taxation of the clergy in dire emergencies at the monarchs' discretion. Following that bull and other actions by Boniface, papal power diminished from its peak under Innocent III's leadership at the beginning of the century. The church was still, however, a formidable institution.

Cathedral and monastic schools had their part in European education, as did the new universities in England, France, Italy, and Switzerland. In 1300, Gothic art and architecture were on the threshold of new forms. Scholasticism was apparent in the work of Anselm, Abelard, and Aquinas. The world was changing.

Multiple-Choice Questions

Choose the best response.

_____ 1. The century between 1152 and 1250 was decisive for both Germany and the papacy because
   a. under its new Hohenstaufen dynasty, Germany immediately collapsed, its rulers more interested in Italy than in Germany itself.
   b. the papacy and the German kings, whom they sometimes crowned emperor, agreed on many issues.
   c. unprecedented legal and institutional growth led to the "papal monarchy."
   d. Conrad III in 1152 designated as his successor his young son, who reigned over a Germany wracked by years close to anarchy.

_____ 2. Frederick, crowned emperor in 1212 by Innocent III,
   a. though Germany cosmopolitan and Germans scintillating.
   b. swore he would not attempt to unite Italy and Germany.
   c. went on both the Second and Third Crusades.
   d. used his considerable energy to unite almost all of Germany.

_____ 3. The Roman Catholic Church in the twelfth century sharpened the tools it used to make its will felt, including
   a. canon law.
   b. the civil law.
   c. the inquisition.
   d. corporal punishment.

_____ 4. The most powerful man ever to hold the papal office up to the twelfth century was
   a. Innocent III.
   b. Leo III.
   c. Boniface VIII.
   d. Henry II.

_____ 5. When he succeeded his brother Richard in 1199, King John of England inherited some problems and quickly created many of his own, including
   a. losing in transit a treasury meant to rescue his brother Richard, kidnapped on his way home from the Crusades.
   b. forging an alliance with Otto IV of Germany.
   c. withholding permission to proceed with elections when bishops died to keep the diocesan incomes.
   d. refusing to accept Innocent III as pope.

_____ 6. Twelfth-century seaborne trade was expanded by the introduction, or wider use, of
   a. the sweep rudder.
   b. the gimbal.
   c. larger ships.
   d. the sexton.

_____ 7. The reformer who called churches brothels and clerics whores, rejected the sacraments, and refused to pay tithes was
   a. Peter Valdes.
   b. Tanchelm of Antwerp.
   c. Francis of Assisi.
   d. Dominic de Gusmán.

_____ 8. The first exclusively women's movement in the history of Christianity was the
   a. Beguines.
   b. Poor Clares.
   c. Cistercians.
   d. Cluny.

_____ 9. Crusading was intended to
   a. create camaraderie between the future monarchs of Europe.
   b. capture the Iberian coast, especially Lisbon.
   c. protect the Holy Land and keep open the pilgrim routes to Jerusalem.
   d. test new sailing vessels that would be used for exploration.

_____ 10. Scholasticism was produced by several related forces, including
   a. a need to distinguish natural philosophy from religion.
   b. the style of intellectual life that resulted from twelfth-century fascination with dogma.
   c. the Christian tradition.
   d. the decline of intellectual interaction between Latin Europe and the Arab and Jewish worlds.

Answers to Multiple-Choice Questions

1. c	3. c	5. c	7. b	9. c
2. b	4. a	6. c	8. a	10. c

Identification

Briefly identify and summarize the historical significance of each of the following:

Hostiensis
Lombard League
Albigensians
Boniface VIII
Philip II
Thomas Aquinas

Peace of Constance
Frederick I Barbarossa
"The Poor Clares"
Magna Carta
Siete Partides
Dante Alighieri

Short-Answer and Essay Questions

11. Discuss the thirteenth-century "kings of genius" in Spain.

12. Analyze the influence of cities and towns in twelfth-century Europe.

13. Discuss the secret of success in Dante's *The Divine Comedy*.

14. Compare the French and German monarchs in the twelfth century.

15. Analyze the twelfth-century crisis between church and state in Europe.

Map Exercise

Map 11.2   The Crusades, 1095–1270

16. On the outline map provided, identify the routes of the later Crusades. What was the purpose of the later Crusades? Why did the Crusades die out after 1300?

Map 11.2 The Crusades, 1095–1270

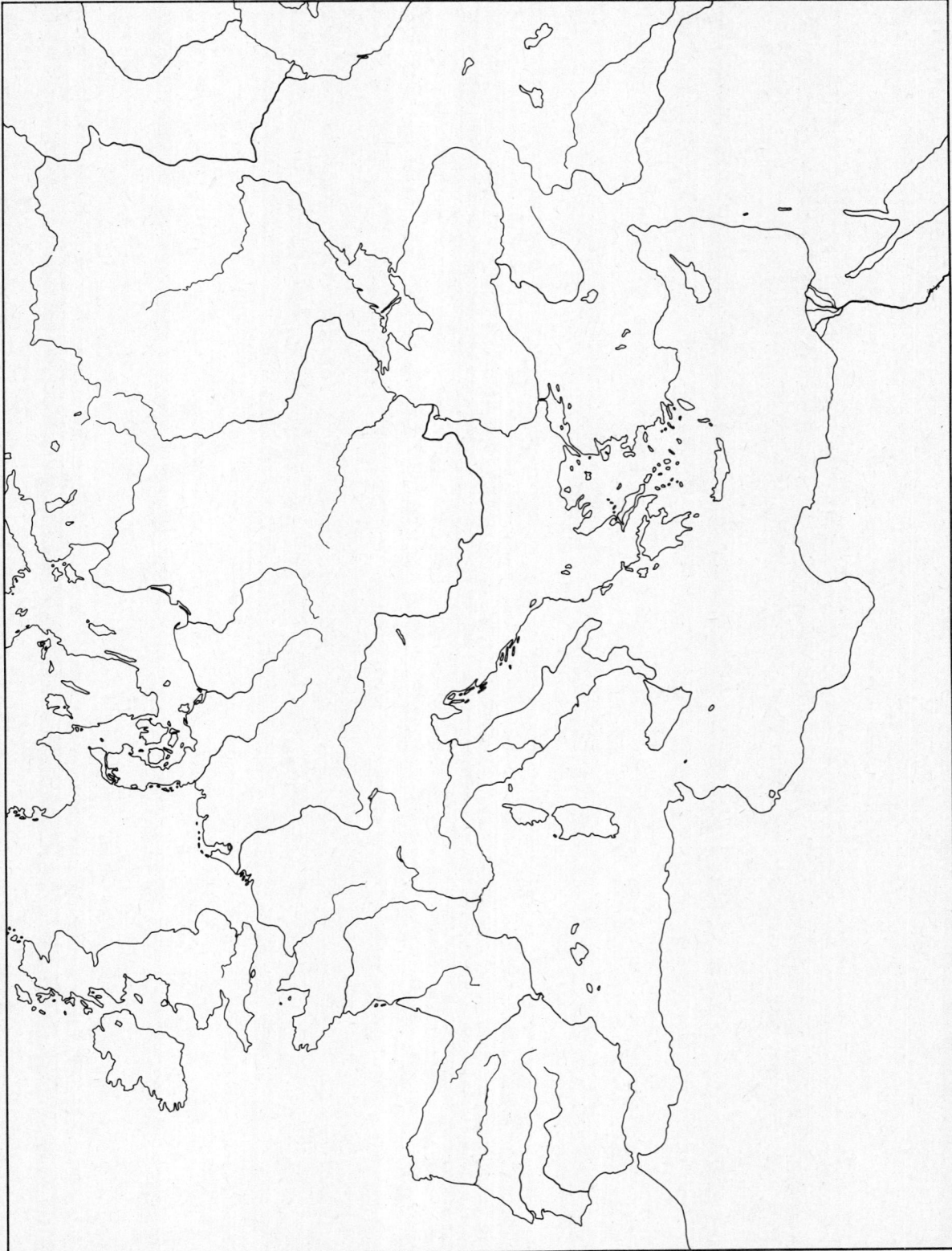

The Late Medieval Crisis in Government and Society

Learning Objectives

After studying this chapter, you should be able to:

1. understand the origins of the Hundred Years' War.

2. analyze the effects of the Hundred Years' War.

3. discuss the crisis in the Western church.

4. describe how the subsistence crisis, the Black Death, and the popular revolts influenced western European economies and societies.

5. discuss the origins of the Holy Roman Empire.

6. understand why tension grew between many European Christians and outsiders.

Summary

The Late Middle Ages was a time of retreat from the growth and expansion experienced during the High Middle Ages. The systems of government formed in the twelfth and thirteenth centuries required strong, charismatic monarchs and short, successful wars. Neither requirement was met.

The Hundred Years' War was an example of the problems facing Late Medieval Europe. A series of short raids and expeditions punctuated by a few significant battles and a number of truces or ineffective treaties, the war began with Edward III's formal declaration in 1340 that he was the king of France. The war can be divided into four stages and lasted until 1453, when the French captured the fortress of Castillon-sur-Dordogne. That final battle ended the hostilities and the war, but without a formal treaty.

The war touched almost all aspects of life in the Late Middle Ages. Though fought between England and France, it sometimes spilled over into Scotland, Castile, Aragon, and the German principalities. Each side took a different view of the Great Schism in the Catholic church and prevented an early settlement of the issue. Paying for the war, particularly for the armies, disrupted business and depleted much of European capital needed for business investment. Finally, the war broke the traditional connection between the French and English nobles and gave rise to nationalist feelings in both states.

The Great Schism—having popes in both Avignon and Rome—raised the issue of ecclesiastical authority for Christian Europeans. By the time the schism was healed, it was clear that papal authority had limits. The fifteenth-century popes would need to fashion a new papal administration and a new explanation for the pope's role in the church and in society.

The great famine in 1315–1322 was a turning point in European life, and so too was the Black Death in 1348 and subsequent years. Both events checked European population growth. Also, particularly the plague, they added to the strains already felt by Europeans and caused social disruption in Europe in the form of violent political and social movements and oppression by Christians of Muslims and Jews. Most of these crises would be solved in the fifteenth century.

Multiple-Choice Questions

Choose the best response.

_____ 1. In fourteenth-century England, resident Justices of the Peace
   a. in practice were royal officials doing the king's bidding.
   b. were modestly well-to-do gentry who were often clients of local magnates.
   c. used their office to carry out projects they felt would benefit all residents in their districts.
   d. worked to help the kings maintain control over their government's financial and judicial machinery.

_____ 2. The Ordinances of 1311
   a. required a greatly diminished role for Parliament.
   b. allowed the King of England to wage war, leave the realm, grant lands or castles, and appoint chief justices and chancellors without approval by the barons in Parliament.
   c. required that the king live off the properties and rights belonging directly to him.
   d. stipulated that complaints about abuses by Parliament would be heard by a commission of royal officials.

_____ 3. The largest kingdom in Christendom in the fourteenth century was
   a. France.
   b. Germany.
   c. England.
   d. Italy.

_____ 4. The Hundred Years' War was
   a. a series of extended battles that turned the conflict into a war of attrition.
   b. dictated by the larger English military.
   c. a series of short raids and expeditions punctuated by a few major battles, truces, and ineffective treaties.
   d. distinctive because of relative cooperation between the English and French monarchs.

_____ 5. Joan of Arc
   a. was condemned and burned at the stake by the French.
   b. almost instantly after her death became a symbol of the French resistance.
   c. despite being condemned as a heretic, was canonized in 1456.
   d. was a minor French military leader not wholly respected by Charles VII's military forces.

_____ 6. The Closing of the Grand Council
   a. was a government attempt to deal with the issue of new citizens in Venice.
   b. guaranteed the political rights of Venetian peasants.
   c. initially decreased the number of families eligible for public office.
   d. elevated political tension within the patriciate to a crisis.

_____ 7. In the bull *Unam sanctam* (1302), Boniface VIII
   a. destroyed the church through his avarice.
   b. declared that there could be no salvation outside the Roman Catholic church.
   c. declared that all ecclesiastical power was derived from the pope and all political power was derived from the monarch.
   d. simplified the procedure by which the faithful could settle ecclesiastical controversies.

_____ 8. The effects of the Great Schism included
   a. courts that cooperated with each other and spent revenues they generated to support each other.
   b. new discussions and debates over church government.
   c. unquestioned acceptance of the pope's position in the church hierarchy.
   d. demands that the pope stand trial before a gathering of his peers.

_____ 9. The great famine in 1315–1322
   a. was caused by unusually hot and dry weather in much of northern Europe.
   b. caused people to die so quickly that no one could keep up with the burials.
   c. began slowly because at the beginning of the crisis cities had enough food stocks to feed their populations.
   d. reduced overpopulation, lessening pressure on resources.

_____ 10. In fourteenth-century Spain, anti-Jewish feelings were
   a. strictly religious.
   b. caused by the movement, after the 1391 attack on Jews in Seville, of Jews to urban areas in Spain.
   c. subsided until antagonism toward Jews began again in Spain late in the fifteenth century.
   d. caused by anger over the economic prominence of some Jewish or *converso* families.

Answers to Multiple-Choice Questions

1. b	3. a	5. b	7. b	9. b
2. c	4. c	6. a	8. b	10. d

Identification

Briefly identify and summarize the historical significance of each of the following:

Peasants' Revolt
The Black Prince
Statutes of Laborers
Martin V
flagellants
Hugh Despenser

Agincourt
Pope John XXII
Salian Law of Succession
Catherine of Sienna
Canterbury Tales
Etienne Marcel

Short-Answer and Essay Questions

11. Summarize the limits on royal power that were evident in the fourteenth century.

12. Discuss the four stages in the Hundred Years' War.

13. Discuss the patterns of economic change in fourteenth-century Europe.

14. Analyze the effects of the Black Death on western Europe.

15. Agree or disagree, wholly or in part, with this statement: "In many respects the years from 1300 to the early fifteenth century were a pause between the growth and expansion of the High Middle Ages and the growth which was to mark the sixteenth century."

Map Exercises

Map 12.1   England and France in the Hundred Years' War

16. Notice the ways in which the boundaries of the English and French holdings changed over the four stages of the war. Why were the English unable to take control of France?

Map 12.3   The Progress of the Black Death

17. On the outline map provided, identify the route by which the Black Death spread through central Italy, southern France, the Low Countries, England, Germany, and the Slavic lands. Why did European doctors have difficulty stemming the spread of the plague?

Map 12.3 The Progress of the Black Death

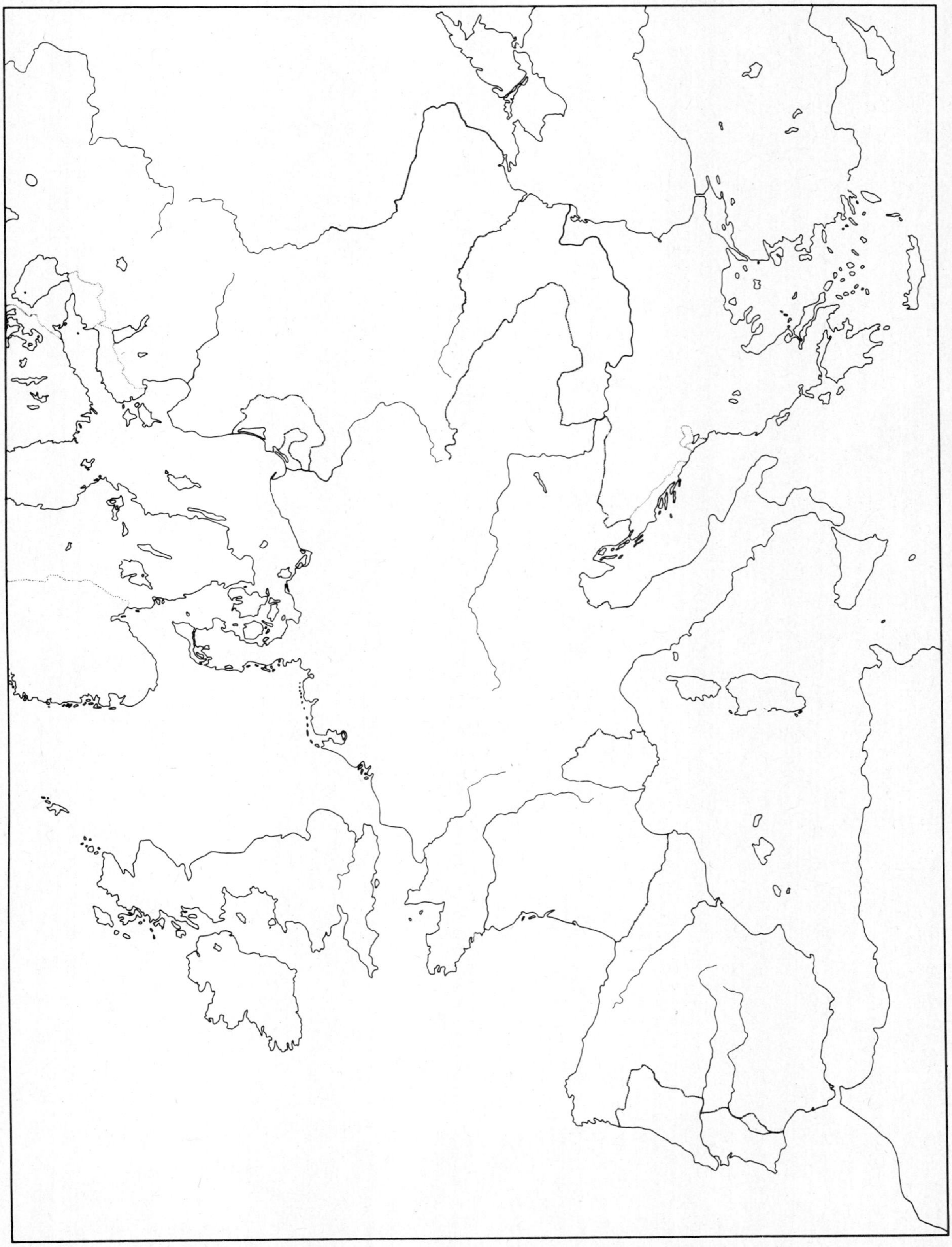

CHAPTER 13

The Late Medieval Recovery

Learning Objectives

After studying this chapter, you should be able to:

1. understand the pattern of economic recovery for the Late Medieval world.
2. discuss Late Medieval Christianity and the Renaissance papacy.
3. understand how the French and English monarchies were reconstructed.
4. discuss the Wars of the Roses.
5. analyze the transformation of the Italian city-states, the triumph of German provincial governments, and the territorial consolidation of northern and eastern Europe.
6. understand how the Ottoman and Spanish Empires were formed.

Summary

The problems of fourteenth-century Europe—Black Death, war, and economic dislocation—had diminished or disappeared by the fifteenth century. That century therefore was a time of recovery for Late Medieval Europe.

Europe experienced an economic revival in the fifteenth century mainly caused by shifts in trade and manufacturing patterns. Italian trade and shipping techniques spread beyond the Mediterranean region and new networks of trade and finance formed. Spain, France, and England became more important players in international trade. Germany, particularly the central region of the state, expanded its influence throughout Central Europe. The decline in population caused by the Great Famine, the Black Death, and fourteenth-century wars profoundly affected agriculture. The new balance of bargaining power favored farmers and laborers. Still, where desirable, Europeans maintained their traditional values.

The Roman Catholic Church responded to its fourteenth-century problems in innovative ways designed to reestablish papal authority and the glory of Rome following the Great Schism, conciliarism, heresy, reform, and local feelings. Nicholas V took the first step in that direction by establishing the church as an important patron of the arts, architecture, and building. The formation of religious brotherhoods or confraternities was the most important local development for individuals and these served as conduits for spiritual growth and political association. Religious houses for women proliferated and outnumbered those for men. They served as economical, safe, and controlled environments for the unmarried or unmarriageable daughters of the wealthy. Kingdoms, provinces, and towns created patron saints. In short, the church worked to provide a definition for belonging and an ideology for public life.

Europeans' political institutions also responded to the crises in the fourteenth century. Local, regional, and national governments learned traditional means of control and adopted them to create stronger institutions. The monarchies in England and France grew in power as the crowns used their courts and the relationship of clientage to secure power over local nobles and officials. On the continent, regional powers took control of administrations in France, Italy, and Germany. The Ottoman Turks became a new power, along with Spain, by toppling the Byzantine Empire in 1453. The marriage of Isabella and Ferdinand precipitated a unifying campaign that would include the Inquisition and sponsorship of Christopher Columbus on a voyage to Asia. At the end of the fifteenth century, Spain was on the verge of becoming a world power. Europe was a dynamic place.

Multiple-Choice Questions

Choose the best response.

_____ 1. Cosimo de Medici solved the problem of unlimited liability that had ruined earlier commercial partnerships by
   a. decentralizing control of the partnerships.
   b. reorganizing the Medici bank of Florence so that all commercial assets of European partners were held at the bank.
   c. creating one partnership for the Medici family.
   d. developing the Medici bank of Florence as a series of bilateral partnerships between himself and easily controlled junior partners in other parts of Europe.

_____ 2. The prosperity of Nuremberg, like that of many of its neighbors, was built *first* on
   a. expanding into international trade.
   b. creating a local marketing network.
   c. cooperation it had with the Medici bank of Florence.
   d. high-interest loans to the nobility by the Fugger family.

_____ 3. Agricultural changes in the Late Medieval period resulted in
   a. lowered rents and increased wages for small farmers and laborers.
   b. high grain prices and relatively low wages.
   c. small farmers subsisting on bread or grain-based gruel with meat, fish, and cheeses only a few times a week.
   d. many landlords giving up raising sheep to concentrate on grain production.

_____ 4. By the late fourteenth century, Christianity
   a. moved away from the question of an individual's salvation and personal relationship to God and the Christian community as the heart of religious practice and theological speculation.
   b. provided a definition of belonging and an ideology for public life for Europeans.
   c. was marked by its leaders' abandonment of their earlier desire to control the laity.
   d. suffered from a decline in the wake of schism, clerical extravagance, and rising national feeling.

_____ 5. The most usual religious practice in the fifteenth century was
    a. flagellation.
    b. developing patron saints for provinces and towns who could protect their clients from natural as well as political disasters.
    c. denouncing the feast of *Corpus Christi*.
    d. membership in religious brotherhoods or confraternities.

_____ 6. Philip the Good held the Banquet of the Oath of the Pheasant in 1454 to
    a. mark his decision to send crusaders to liberate Constantinople.
    b. celebrate his humility in the eyes of God.
    c. vow on a live pheasant that the Crusades were officially finished.
    d. mark his return from a successful Crusade to liberate Jerusalem from the Turks.

_____ 7. To end the war with the English and revive royal power in France was the reason for the changed behavior of King Charles VII. By the late 1430s, Charles had
    a. failed to learn how to handle the political factions that had riven the French court.
    b. made careful appointments and judiciously offered annuities and honors in a successful effort to draw his nobility to the royal court as well as make them dependent on it.
    c. solidified his power by taking advantage of his charisma and a widespread desire for war.
    d. given up his right to collect direct taxes.

_____ 8. By the time Henry VII died in 1509, the English monarchy was more powerful than it had been at any time for the past century, mainly because Henry
    a. created a seemingly informal court.
    b. carefully saved his funds.
    c. controlled local affairs through the traditional system of royal patronage.
    d. transformed the institutions of government.

_____ 9. Control of the traditional Papal State was the key to papal independence. To maintain that control, papal administrators
    a. worked to dismantle the system of nepotism that had flourished in the papal bureaucracy.
    b. worked to regain jurisdiction over towns and regions that had become nearly autonomous and allies of other regional powers.
    c. lauded the excesses of Alexander VI, whom contemporaries accused of buying the papal election.
    d. sought posts in papal territories for papal offspring.

_____ 10. The sack of Constantinople in 1453 by the Muslim Ottoman Turks
    a. ultimately caused the Turks to relinquish Anatolia.
    b. caused Turks to feel sympathy for the vanquished Christians and their fallen leader, Emperor Constantine XI.
    c. sent shock waves through Christian Europe and brought forth calls for new Crusades to liberate the East from the evils of Islam.
    d. represented the end of the profound clash between Christian and Muslim civilizations.

Answers to Multiple-Choice Questions

1. d	3. a	5. d	7. b	9. b
2. b	4. b	6. a	8. c	10. c

Identification

Briefly identify and summarize the historical significance of each of the following:

Geert Groote
Summa of Arithmetic Techniques
Sultan Mehmed II
Hanseatic League
Ivan III
On Architecture
Giovanni de Medici

Nicholas V
Jan Van Eyck
Frederick III
Richard III
Margery Kemp
San Bernardino of Siena

Short-Answer and Essay Questions

11. Summarize the causes of the European economic revival in the fifteenth century.

12. Discuss the transformation of cloth manufacture in Late Medieval Europe.

13. Summarize women's part in the religious life of the Late Medieval world.

14. Analyze the causes and results of the English Wars of the Roses.

15. Analyze the ways in which Europe at the end of the fifteenth century was profoundly different than it had been in the middle of the fourteenth.

Map Exercise

Map 13.3   Turkey and Eastern Europe

16. On the outline map provided, identify the trade zones in Europe and the Mediterranean. How did the development of new trade zones affect the power of the Hanseatic League?

(Note: the outline map differs from the map in the main text.)

Map 13.3 Turkey and Eastern Europe

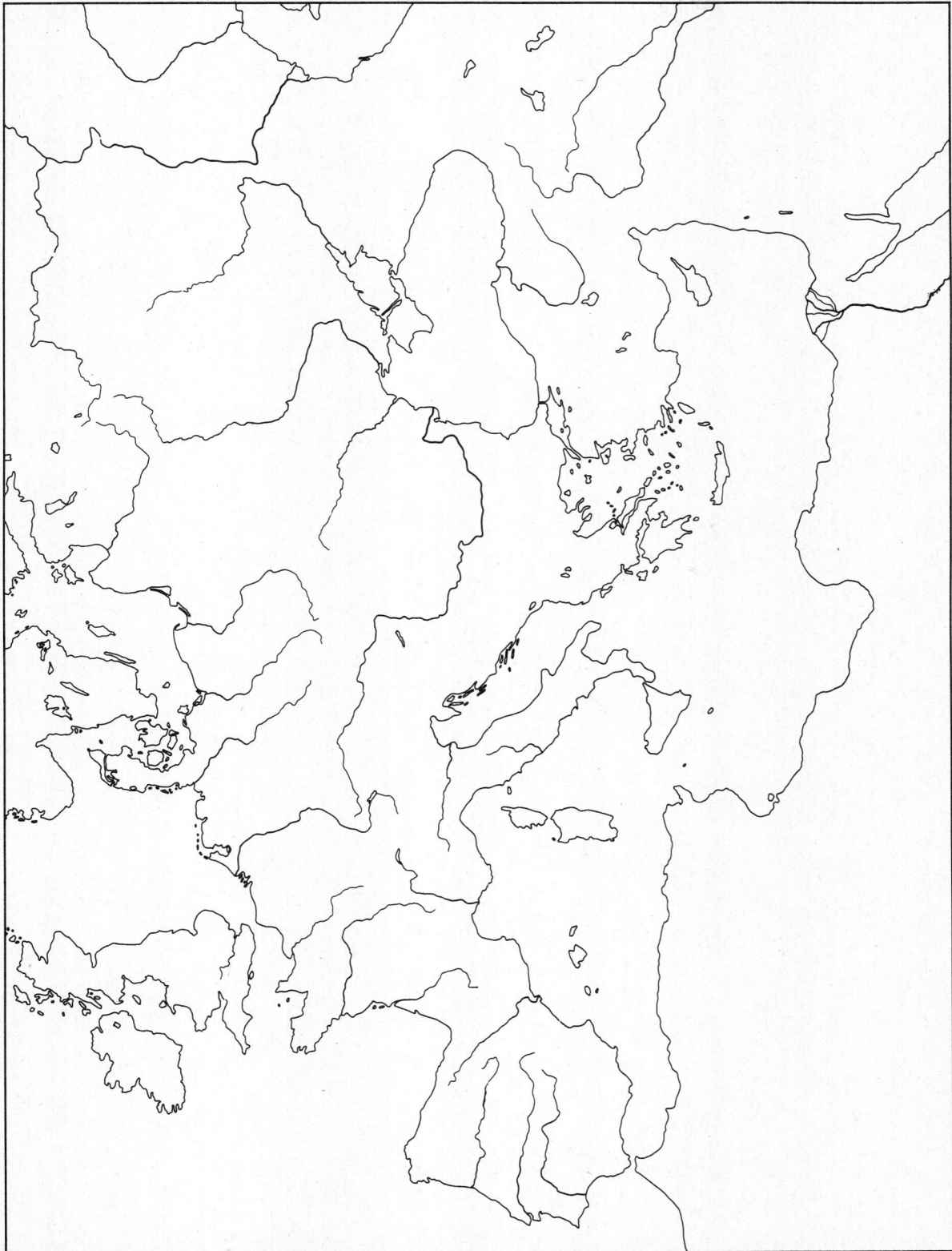

CHAPTER 14

The Renaissance

Learning Objectives

After studying this chapter, you should be able to:

1. understand how the growing European economy and population found expression in joyous enthusiasm for life.

2. discuss art and architecture in the Italian Renaissance.

3. understand why the Renaissance began in Italy.

4. discuss the meaning of humanism and its importance for Western education and thought.

5. analyze how the Renaissance spread outside Italy.

Summary

The Renaissance in the fourteenth through sixteenth centuries was the second remaking of European culture. The first had occurred between the eleventh and thirteenth centuries. At that time a growing European economy and population had found an optimistic joy in life. Europeans had reshaped their lives. They had extended Christianity and the church to all corners of Europe, and they had created strong institutions in the university, independent towns, and the dynastic states of France and England.

The second rebirth was a bit more cynical than the first. For all the recovery in the fifteenth century, the church was mired in corruption and apathy. For many Europeans it had become an obstacle to religious feeling. Older universities had come under attack as Europeans questioned the legitimacy of the curriculum and the quality of education received by students who attended the institutions. European rulers continued aggressive campaigns to consolidate their power. And a resurgence of the plague reminded Europeans just how fragile life was. Still, the Renaissance flourished until religious warfare in the sixteenth century cut it off.

The Renaissance began in Italy. Its northern urban areas provided cosmopolitan centers where people could freely exchange ideas, information, and products. The worldliness of Italian culture was already established, and Italians had only to look around them to see the remnants of an ancient civilization greater than their own. Italy had recovered from the plague faster than the rest of Europe and, for the first time, had the wealth to spend on reclaiming their ancient culture.

The concept of *virtù* permeated Italian Renaissance society. It spread to other parts of Europe and in subtle ways transformed the traditional values of deference and obedience. In northern Italy, specifically Florence, *virtù* was closely associated with civic responsibilities. The bold, intelligent Renaissance Man was expected to devote at least some of his energies to his community.

Renaissance Italians admired versatility and individual brilliance. They expected every man who sought public acclaim to attempt intellectual and artistic pursuits as well as practical activities such as business, hunting, and warfare. The two most famous Renaissance Men were Leonardo da Vinci and Michelangelo.

Italy provided the prototype for the Renaissance Man. Outside Italy, the most important contribution to the Renaissance other than movable type was the Christian Humanism movement. It was Italian in origin but reached its peak outside Italy. Christian Humanists were interested in modernizing Medieval Christianity. Renaissance Humanism in general was a broad movement whose adherents admired classical culture. Humanists brought about reform in secondary education that would last until the twentieth century, introduced Greek studies to the West, and powerfully influenced historical development.

Beyond its cultural achievements, Renaissance Europe was notorious for its increasingly elaborate and sumptuous courts. For European rulers, these courts were one way of creating a unified ideology and culture and solidifying their bureaucratic and political power, which had been growing since the fourteenth century.

Multiple-Choice Questions

Choose the best response.

_____ 1. The word "Renaissance" names
   a. the Italian recovery from the fourteenth-century devastation of the Black Death.
   b. the growing European economy and population late in the thirteenth century.
   c. the rediscovery of art and literature that had died out during the Medieval era.
   d. the intellectual and cultural developments that began in Italy around the mid-fourteenth century.

_____ 2. The Renaissance began in Italy because
   a. its northern region had a greater concentration of rural areas that made it easier for a new culture to spread.
   b. Italians had only to look at their classical past for remnants of a civilization greater than their own.
   c. slower recovery from the Black Death meant Italian aristocrats spent more money on culture and art to offer hope of a better life to Italian peasants.
   d. the church encouraged individuals to recognize freedom of religion, guild, community, and family.

_____ 3. The Humanists
   a. denounced Greek studies and Greek manuscripts and instead focused on reviving Roman literature.
   b. provided the West with a uniform body of knowledge learned by almost all educated men for hundreds of years.
   c. believed that occupational education was more important than liberal education.
   d. believed that a classical education could lead only to the decline of Western civilization.

_____ 4. The most versatile artist in the Renaissance, and the most difficult to classify, was
a. Michelangelo.
b. Donatello.
c. Raphael.
d. Leonardo da Vinci.

_____ 5. Renaissance culture was most thoroughly manipulated for political purposes at
a. the court of Mantua.
b. the papal state.
c. Sistine Chapel.
d. Venice.

_____ 6. The increasingly elaborate and sumptuous courts in the late fourteenth and fifteenth centuries
a. hastened the end of the Renaissance.
b. created a number of prestigious offices that were not particularly lucrative.
c. lost their interest in chivalric values, as in Arthurian romances.
d. served as a means for rulers to create a unified culture and ideology.

_____ 7. Renaissance ideas
a. were spread exclusively in intellectual circles.
b. were part of the transformation of the medieval knight into the early modern "gentleman."
c. were debated by groups who were no longer interested in such topics as nobility, humor, women, and love.
d. were fundamentally atheistic.

_____ 8. Miguel de Cervantes satirized medieval chivalry and analyzed life in sixteenth-century Spain in
a. _Doctor Faustus._
b. _The Adoration of the Mystic Lamb._
c. _Don Quixote._
d. _Praise of Folly._

_____ 9. Northern Renaissance art
a. normally combined Christian subjects with new naturalism.
b. focused solely on Christian subjects.
c. focused mainly on new naturalism.
d. blended earlier styles with revolutionary Italian ideas.

_____ 10. The concept of _virtù_
a. was used as a standard for behavior in Italy, but did not spread to the rest of Europe.
b. spread throughout Europe, subtly changing the traditional values of deference and obedience.
c. is positively related to _fortuna_ in Renaissance Europe.
d. opposed the idea that the bold, intelligent man was expected to devote some of his energies to his community.

Answers to Multiple-Choice Questions

1. d	3. b	5. a	7. b	9. a
2. b	4. d	6. d	8. c	10. b

Identification

Briefly identify and summarize the historical significance of each of the following:

Michelangelo   *The Book of the Courtier*
Andrea Mantegna   *Praise of Folly*
François Rabelais   Isabella d'Este
Christopher Marlowe   Pisanello
Machiavelli   Petrarch

Short-Answer and Essay Questions

11. Summarize how Renaissance culture was most thoroughly manipulated at the court of the Gonzaga in Mantua.

12. Compare the writings of François Rabelais with those of Baldassare Castiglione.

13. Apart from movable type, what was the most important European contribution (outside Italy) to the Renaissance? Why is this the most important innovation?

14. Why did the Renaissance innovations depend on study of the past?

15. Did economic and political factors or individual genius determine the course the Renaissance would follow in Europe?

Map Exercise

Map 14.1   The Spread of Printing

16. On the outline map provided, identify the areas in Europe where the Renaissance began and those to which it later spread. Why did the Renaissance begin where it did? Could it have begun elsewhere?

Map 14.1 The Spread of Printing

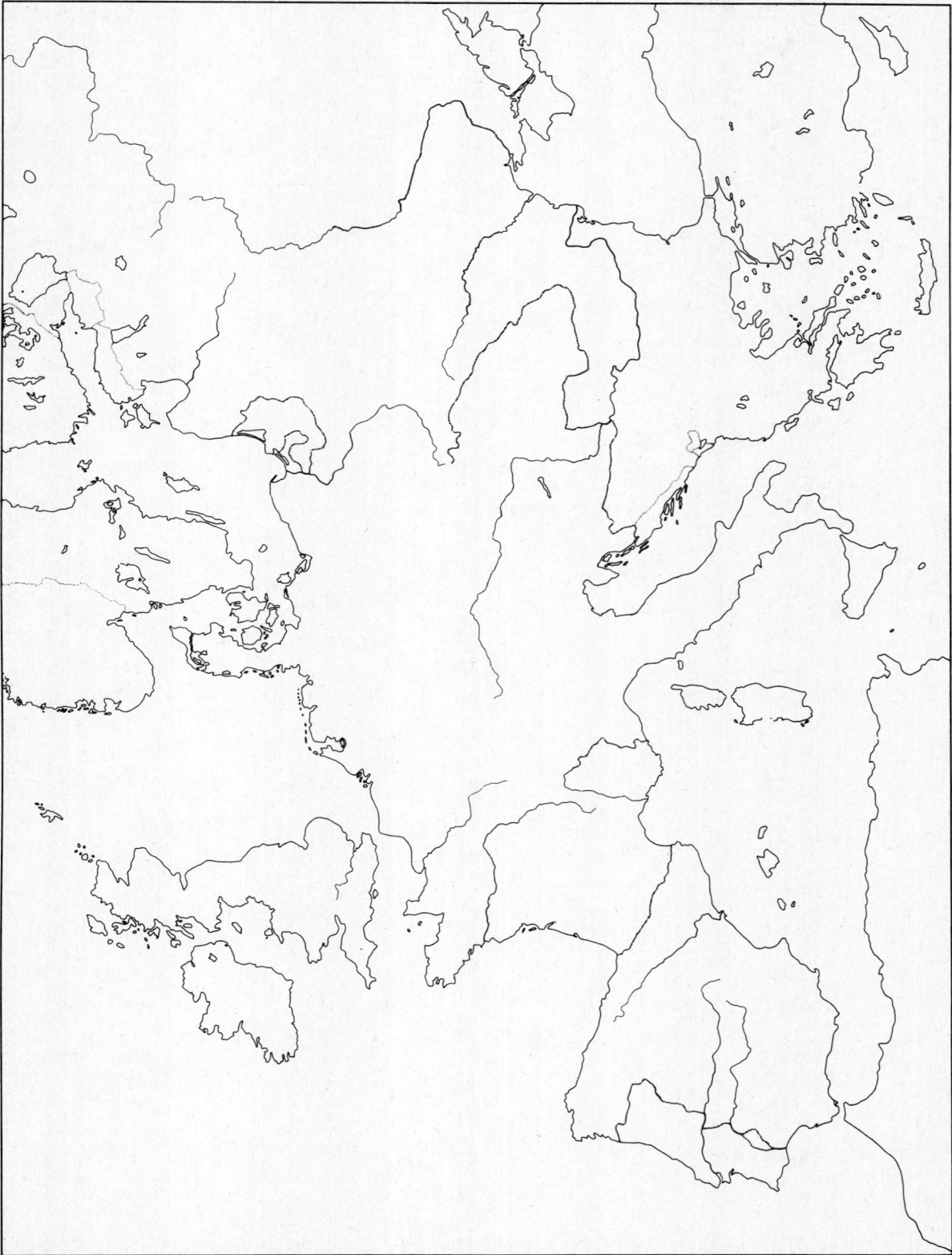

CHAPTER 15

Europe, the Old World and the New

Learning Objectives

After studying this chapter, you should be able to:

1. describe how the innovations in navigation and the "geographic" revolution in the fifteenth century helped to contribute to European expansion.

2. discuss the political and economic changes in Western Europe during the fifteenth century and analyze how these forces contributed to European expansion.

3. understand the origins and development of Portuguese exploration, discovery, and expansion and their effect on Italian (Venetian) trade with the Orient.

4. understand the relationship between Spain's Reconquista and its acquisition of an overseas empire.

5. define the price revolution and how it affected European expansion in the fifteenth and sixteenth centuries.

6. compare the Spanish voyages of discovery with those of their Iberian rival, the Portuguese.

7. describe the pre-Columbian world of native Americans.

8. understand the motives of the Spanish *conquistadores* and the type and structure of empire they established for Spain in the New World.

9. describe how conquest affected both culture and environment of native Americans.

10. discuss how the Iberian conquest of the New World intensified Old World rivalries.

Summary

In the early modern period, explorers representing western European nations crossed immense oceans to discover other civilizations. With superior material and technological strength, especially firearms, Europeans were able to conquer other peoples, some even more advanced than themselves in some areas of development. The motives for empire and expansion varied from desire to serve God, to glory, gold, and even "geopolitics"—combined geographic and political ambitions.

Prince Henry the Navigator of Portugal personally directed much of his nation's early exploration to promote commerce, national power, and Christianity. In 1488, Bartholomeu Dias rounded the Cape of Good Hope, and by 1497 Vasco da Gama had reached India by sea. Soon after, Portugal acquired dominance in trade with the East—a position once controlled by the Italians (most notably the Venetians), Byzantines, and Arabs.

Europeans generally disdained Oriental culture. Taking advantage of military and political disunity in India, western Europeans dominated the subcontinent with relatively few people. In India, Europeans found an entrenched caste system. Farther east in China, they found an ancient civilization that had endured many changes. The Chinese emperor, with an efficient, well-trained bureaucracy run by mandarins, ruled a vast empire firmly built on communal villages.

Portugal established its trading empire on mercantilist principles, establishing the rule that the mother country should supply manufactured goods in exchange for raw materials from its colony. Other nations were excluded from the trading monopoly that the mother country established. Eventually, all European powers with colonial possessions in the New World and the Far East subscribed to mercantile theory. Despite their head start, the Portuguese were challenged late in the sixteenth and early in the seventeenth centuries by the French, Dutch, and English, eventually losing their dominance in the East.

In 1492, Columbus, an experienced voyager, discovered a "New World" that he claimed for Spain. Discoveries multiplied after Columbus's initial voyage, especially as Spanish explorers hunted for a northwest or southwest passage around the Americas.

Soon after the explorers came the infamous Spanish *conquistadores*. Led by such men as Hernán Cortés and Juan Pizarro, warriors fresh from their nation's Reconquista, Spain soon had a huge empire in the Americas. Spain established a centralized administration in its New World colonies with a viceroy representing the Crown. Native Americans were converted to Christianity, often by force, but eventually came under protection by the Catholic Church under the New Laws of 1542. Nevertheless, millions of native Americans died of European diseases and brutal treatment.

Led by the Portuguese and Spanish, by the end of the sixteenth century the patterns were set for conquering and exploiting the rest of the New World. This first phase established the horrible slave trade involving both native Americans and Africans, for exterminating the native populations, and for destroying centuries-old social arrangements. New products as well as knowledge of other beliefs and institutions created a new world in the West. Expansion revolutionized western European economies and societies. As Portugal and Spain explored Africa, Asia, and the New World, they set the stage for international politics for centuries to come.

Multiple-Choice Questions

Choose the best response.

_____ 1. Which was a cause of the age of exploration?
  a. The Russians' continued encroachment into central Europe
  b. Technological backwardness making long sea voyages risky
  c. Ottoman expansion offering access to Eastern goods
  d. European demand for Eastern spices

_____ 2. Which of these best exemplifies the age of exploration?
  a. Crusaders establishing feudal kingdoms in the Near East
  b. Genoa and Venice establishing commercial ports in the Mediterranean
  c. Sailing around Africa to reach the rich trading centers in India
  d. Trading with the Muslim empires in the Middle East for slaves and gold

_____ 3. The first country to discover an all-water route to India was
    a. Spain.
    b. Portugal.
    c. France.
    d. England.

_____ 4. By the end of the sixteenth century, Portugal had
    a. overextended its empire and fallen out of the European exploration race.
    b. become one of the trading capitals of the world.
    c. become involved in a costly war with the Ottomans to dominate the spice trade.
    d. allied with England and Spain to ensure domination in the East.

_____ 5. For more than a thousand years, educated Europeans thought of the world as it had been described in the second century by
    a. Nerva.
    b. Plato.
    c. Ptolemy.
    d. Marco Polo.

_____ 6. The legendary ruler of a Christian kingdom in the heart of Africa was
    a. Cortés.
    b. Pizarro.
    c. Henry the Navigator.
    d. Prester John.

_____ 7. Until the eighteenth century, the largest and richest overseas empire was that established by
    a. Spain.
    b. Portugal.
    c. England.
    d. France.

_____ 8. During the Middle Ages, the spice trade with India was monopolized by
    a. Spaniards and Portuguese.
    b. Muslims and Venetians.
    c. Byzantines and Russians.
    d. French and English.

_____ 9. Ferdinand Magellan
    a. circumnavigated the globe.
    b. reached India by sailing around Africa.
    c. discovered Brazil.
    d. conquered Peru.

_____ 10. The conqueror of the Aztecs was
    a. Pizarro.
    b. Cortés.
    c. Vasco da Gama.
    d. Bartholomeu Dias.

Answers to Multiple-Choice Questions

1. d	3. b	5. c	7. a	9. a
2. c	4. a	6. d	8. b	10. b

Identification

Briefly identify and summarize the historical significance of each of the following:

encomiendas   Prince Henry the Navigator
Marco Polo   The New Laws of 1542
Cortés   Moctezuma
Juan de Sepulveda   Magellan
Bartolomé de las Casas   Pizarro

Short-Answer and Essay Questions

11. What forces promoted European expansion?

12. Why were Europeans able to overcome non-Europeans in the New World?

13. What role did each of these have during the age of exploration? Hernán Cortés, Bartolomé de las Casas, Vasco da Gama.

14. Discuss the various myths surrounding Columbus and his famed voyage.

15. Describe the differences between Aztecs and Incas.

Map Exercise

Map 15.2 World Exploration
Map 15.3 Mexico and Central America
Map 15.4 Peru and Central America

16. On the outline map provided, and referring to maps 15.2, 15.3, and 15.4, mark the exploration routes of da Gama, Columbus, and Magellan; also show Cueta, the Cape of Good Hope, Amsterdam, Guinea, Cape Horn, London, Lisbon, Goa, Paris, and the Aztec and Inca empires in the New World.

Map 15.2 World Exploration
Map 15.3 Mexico and Central America
Map 15.4 Peru and Central America

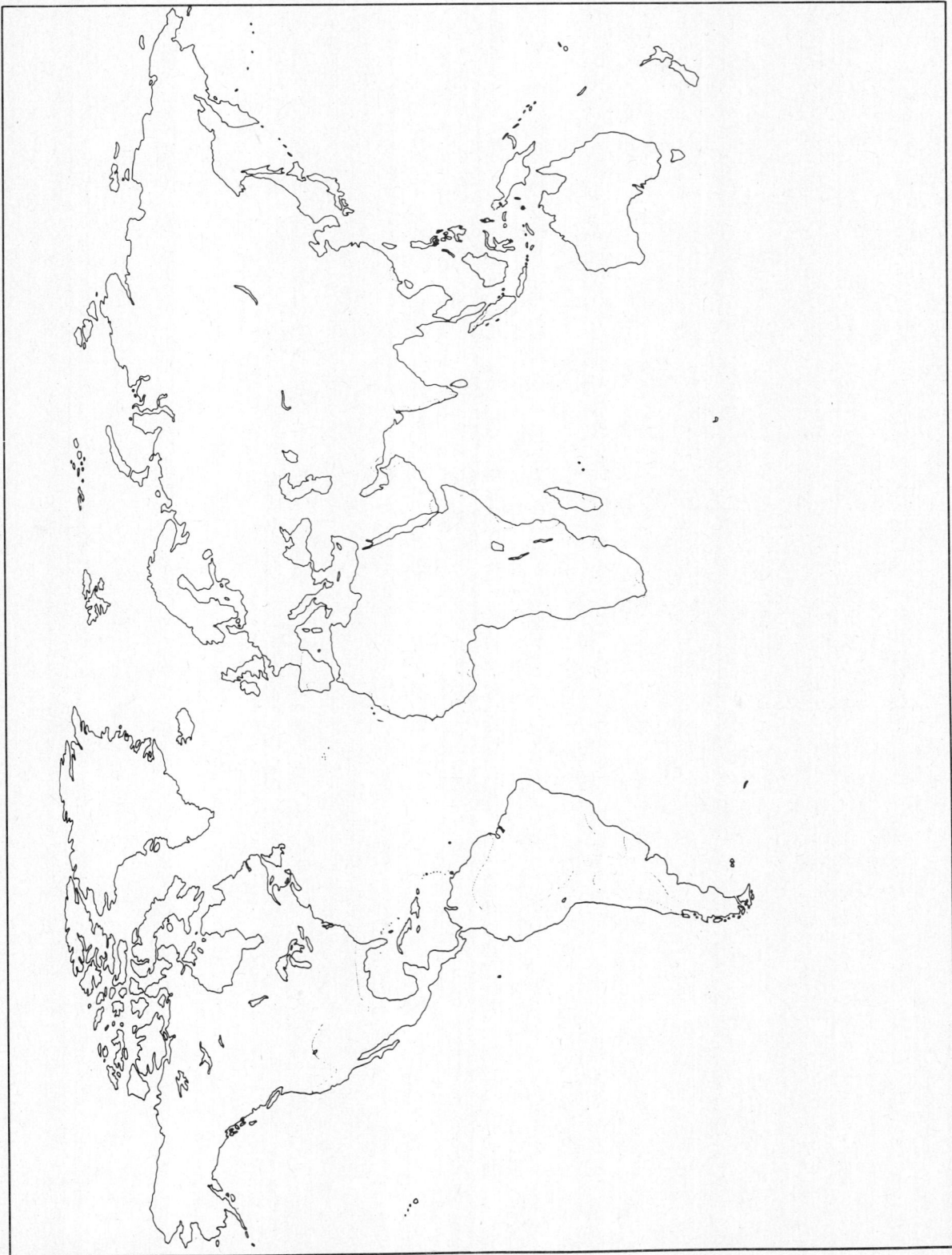

The Reformation

Learning Objectives

After studying this chapter, you should be able to:

1. explain to whom Luther's ideas appealed, and why they did.

2. describe how the conflict between Catholics and Lutherans in the Holy Roman Empire came out.

3. understand Luther's political and social views and be able to apply them to the Peasants' Revolt.

4. analyze the beliefs of John Calvin, especially his views on salvation.

5. explain Calvinism's social and political implications, and why, despite their seeming harshness, they succeeded in converting thousands to the faith.

6. discuss the Reformation's influence on France and how the movement was related to political issues and conflict.

7. explain the causes of the English Reformation, and describe the religious, economic, and political changes resulting from the break with Rome.

8. discuss the Roman Catholic reaction to the Reformation and how the church attempted to defend itself and fight Protestantism in Europe.

9. describe the ways in which the Reformation contributed to the further breakup of the medieval world and the coming of the modern age.

Summary

In 1517, Martin Luther began a profoundly important revolution when he nailed his Ninety-Five Theses on the door of the University of Wittenberg, where he taught theology. In his theses, Luther questioned an array of Catholic Church practices, but the one that angered him most was the granting of indulgences—an act popularly believed to bestow forgiveness of sin and remission of punishment. Luther himself had come to believe in the primacy of faith over good works and in the priesthood of individual believers.

Luther's challenge produced an upheaval within the church, eventually driving him to reject most Catholic doctrine and ritual and organize his own church. Excommunicated in 1521, Luther became a national hero among many northern German princes and their subjects, who had long felt alienated and oppressed by the Italian-controlled Roman church. Soon after Luther came under protection by the elector of Saxony, other German princes joined the Protestant revolt. The Reformation had begun.

Luther owed his success partly to religious sentiment and partly to political issues that had been festering between many of the German princes and the papacy since the Middle Ages. Luther's new Protestant theology, especially his doctrine of justification by faith, had wide appeal among a German population that had been disenchanted with Catholic worship for some time.

Although Holy Roman Emperor Charles V fought Protestantism, he was distracted by the many other problems in his massive empire. In 1555, after several years trying to crush the Protestant revolt, Charles was forced to accept the Peace of Augsburg if he hoped to restore peace to his wartorn empire. The settlement recognized the right of each prince to determine whether his lands would be Catholic or Lutheran; it did not, however, recognize any other Protestant groups.

Meanwhile, other Protestant groups formed, such as Ulrich Zwingli's and John Calvin's respective movements in Switzerland. Both men reinforced fundamental Protestant tenets while promoting the simplicity of primitive Christianity and rejecting Catholic liturgy. Calvin's influence was greater than that of Zwingli, for his brand of Protestantism spread rapidly across western Europe to France, Scotland, and England, converting thousands in those countries to Calvinism. Calvinism rejected the Catholic emphasis on salvation, establishing instead the doctrine of predestination—that only a very few, the "elect," had been chosen by God to be saved. Although Calvinism was not originally a very democratic faith, its preaching set the individual above the state and eventually contributed to modern democratic thought.

The English Reformation was carried out by royal authority. By the Act of Supremacy in 1534, Henry VIII became head of the English church. He retained Catholic doctrine and ritual but ended Rome's authority over all aspects of the Church of England. Henry benefited from support by the middle and upper classes, for his seizure of monastic lands and dissolution of monasteries allowed many members of these classes to gain economically.

At first the Catholic Church responded to the Protestant challenge by trying to suppress the revolt militarily. When that failed, the church then rallied to reform itself from within, an effort known today as the Catholic Reformation. The Habsburg monarchs in Spain and Germany actively led the Catholic Reformation, finding a great boon to their cause in a new religious order, the Society of Jesus, or Jesuits, founded in the 1540s by Ignatius Loyola. Loyola organized the Jesuits on the lines of strict military discipline, and, because of their devotion to church and pope, won back some lands from Protestantism and made converts overseas.

The Council of Trent, convened in 1545, brought about reform but also reaffirmed Catholic doctrine and papal supremacy, ending the hope of some Catholics for compromise with Protestants. The Catholic Reformation succeeded in stemming the tide of Protestantism. Thus, by 1580 the lines of Catholic and Protestant lands in Europe were drawn.

Multiple-Choice Questions

Choose the best response.

_____ 1. The starting point for the Reformation was
    a. *On Christian Liberty.*
    b. assassination of the pope.
    c. Ninety-Five Theses.
    d. rejection of transubstantiation.

_____ 2. The cause of the Protestant Reformation was a dispute about
   a. whether priests could marry.
   b. how to control the rampant practice of nepotism among church officials.
   c. the selling of indulgences.
   d. the need to simplify church ritual and adornment.

_____ 3. Luther's attack on indulgences was precipitated by the actions of
   a. John Eck.
   b. Tetzel.
   c. Charles V.
   d. Frederick of Saxony.

_____ 4. An analysis of Luther's career shows that he
   a. recognized good works and the sacraments as the primary means of attaining salvation.
   b. referred to the pope as an Antichrist.
   c. considered Frederick of Saxony his worst enemy.
   d. was condemned as a heretic—an ecclesiastical offense—but was never condemned by civil authorities.

_____ 5. Justification by faith alone can best be associated with
   a. the constitution developed by the Genevan theocracy.
   b. Luther's contribution to the new theology.
   c. the battle cry of the Anabaptists.
   d. Ignatius Loyola.

_____ 6. Luther's reaction to growing social unrest among the peasants involved
   a. a reminder that the clergy must still interpret the Bible.
   b. urging them to seek indulgences and pray for their souls.
   c. encouraging them to fast and make pilgrimages to help them resign themselves to their lives.
   d. his supporting the nobility's suppression of the peasants.

_____ 7. Those massacred on Saint Bartholomew's Day were
   a. Catholics.
   b. Jews.
   c. French Calvinists.
   d. Anabaptists.

_____ 8. Which one of these countries remained overwhelmingly Catholic?
   a. England.
   b. France.
   c. Spain.
   d. Germany.

_____ 9. Which of these was related to the Anabaptists?
   a. The St. Bartholomew's Day Massacre
   b. The capture of the city of Münster
   c. Civil war in France
   d. The Peasants' Revolt in Germany

_____ 10. It would be most accurate to describe the English Reformation as
   a. the result of Henry VIII's insistence that the church stiffen its position on divorce.
   b. supported by the lesser nobility and gentry, who benefited economically from the break with Rome.
   c. stemming from English preference for Roman primacy over the English church.
   d. a peaceful movement that allowed the church to retain much of its political and economic power in England.

Answers to Multiple-Choice Questions

1. c	3. b	5. b	7. c	9. b
2. c	4. b	6. d	8. c	10. b

Identification

Briefly identify and summarize the historical significance of each of the following:

indulgences
Anabaptists
Ninety-Five Theses
Peasants' Revolt
Ignatius Loyola

Ulrich Zwingli
John Calvin
Catherine of Aragon
Charles V
Peace of Augsburg

Short-Answer and Essay Questions

11. Why did Luther attack the sale of indulgences?

12. What was the relationship between the Reformation and the Peasants' Revolt?

13. Trace the major elements in the Catholic Counter-Reformation.

14. What were the political and social implications of Calvinism?

15. Describe the new Protestant theology of Luther and Calvin and how their beliefs differed from those of traditional Catholicism.

Map Exercise

Map 16.1 Reform in Germany
Map 16.2 Protestants and Catholics in 1555

16. On the outline map provided, and using maps 16.1 and 16.2 in the textbook as reference, outline and locate these areas: the Holy Roman Empire and its main regions—Bohemia, the Spanish Netherlands, Poland, France, Hungary, and Austria. Also within the empire, locate some of the major cities where Protestants were in control. Shade in those areas of the Continent which by 1555 were either predominantly Protestant nations or areas, and those which remained Catholic. Also locate the Ottoman empire.

Map 16.1 Reform in Germany
Map 16.2 Protestants and Catholics in 1555

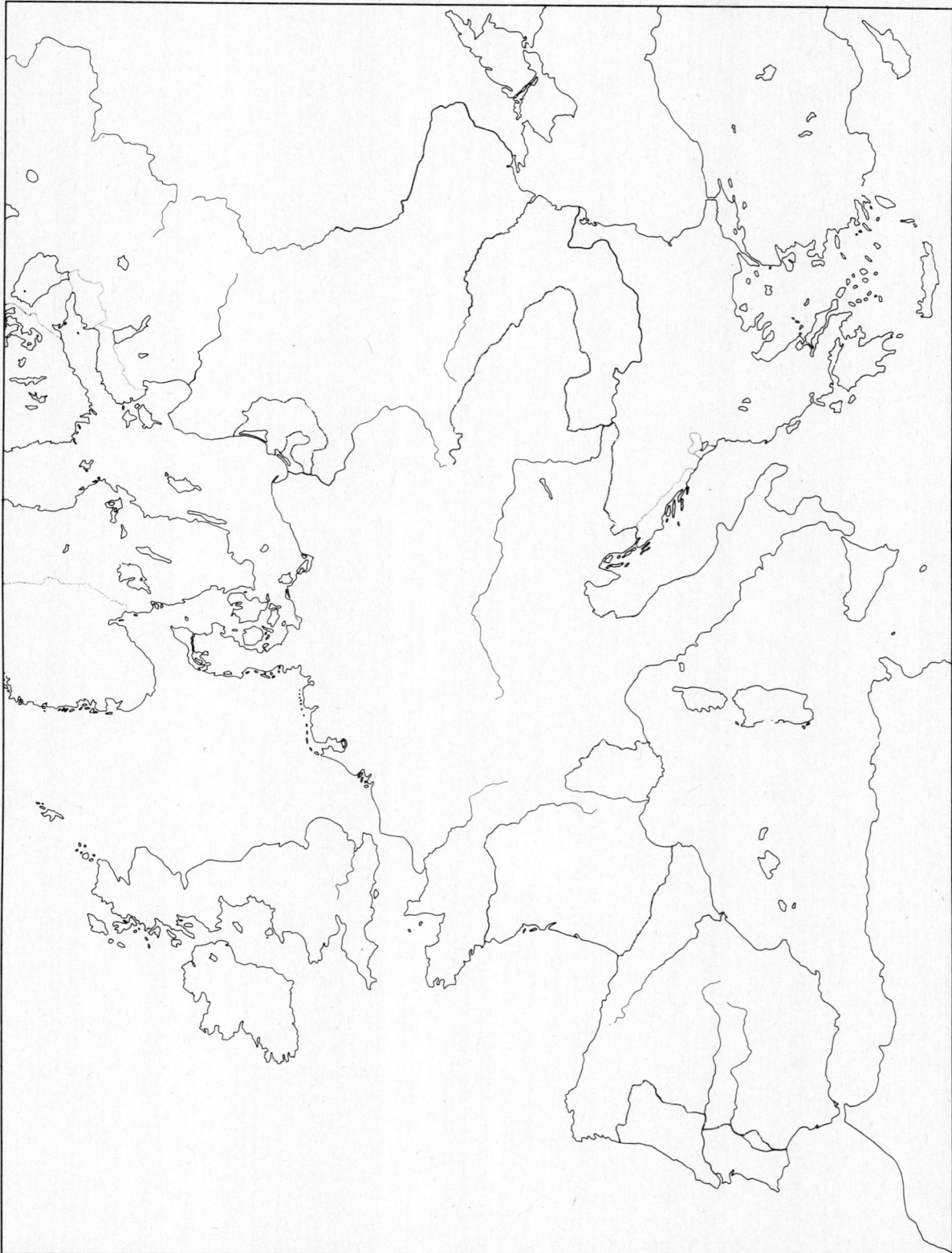

CHAPTER 17

Europe in the Age of Philip II, 1559–1600

Learning Objectives

After studying this chapter, you should be able to:

1. trace the formation of national states in the early modern period, describing their major characteristics and the importance of religious and economic factors in their development.

2. account for both the power and weakness Spain demonstrated from the time of Charles V (king of Spain and Holy Roman emperor) through the reign of his son Philip II.

3. describe the French monarchy from the reign of Francis I through that of Henry IV, especially the effect of the French civil and religious wars in the middle sixteenth century and how these helped consolidate monarchial power.

4. analyze the development of the English national state during the reign of the Tudors, especially the effects of religious conflict in English political affairs.

5. account for the failure of a unified national state to form in Germany, though legitimate nation-states did appear in eastern Europe, most notably Russia and Poland.

6. understand the structure and content of European society in the sixteenth century, especially the important economic changes in western Europe that affected the social order.

7. understand the social and cultural changes that occurred during the sixteenth century, especially in education, literature, and political theory, which reflected a more secular or "humanistic" outlook.

Summary

During the sixteenth century, political, social, economic and intellectual (primarily literary) changes were beginning the "modern" period. The modern state system of nation-states—Spain, France, and England—competed for dominance in western Europe. A new idea that arose with them was nationalism. European states also built diplomatic services and professional armies and the first modern navies. Increasing population, trade, and prices heightened already tense political and religious relations among the European powers, leading to warfare.

Philip II of Spain waged constant war against Protestantism, France, the Ottoman Turks, and his subjects in the Netherlands. The Dutch revolted against Philip's attempt to limit their autonomy and to use the inquisition against Protestants. During a long, costly war the northern provinces (the present Holland) declared their independence from Spain. Elizabeth I helped the Dutch, enraging Philip, who launched an armada to invade and conquer England. Stormy weather and the English navy saved England from invasion, instead inflicting upon Spain its most humiliating and fateful defeat, a turning point for Spain (gradual international decline) and for England (improved international standing).

In Spain as elsewhere, growing absolutism brought persistent struggles against local centers of power. Philip centralized administration and reduced the power of the Cortes, the representative assemblies. And yet, Spain failed to establish a sound economic basis for its power. Despite New World bullion, the Spanish economy stagnated—Philip's incessant warfare drained the nation's treasury.

In the sixteenth century, France was plunged into nearly fifty years of civil and religious strife. Although the French Catholic Church successfully resisted the first generation of Protestant reformers, Calvinist pastors converted nearly 10 percent of the population and more than 30 percent of the nobility by 1560. Political instability following Henry II's death in 1559 encouraged rival aristocratic families and bloody civil war in 1562 culminated in the Saint Bartholomew's Day Massacre in 1572. Henry IV, by the Edict of Nantes (1598), assured the Huguenots of some religious toleration. Religious passions diminished, and the French monarchy recovered its strength.

In England, Henry VIII moved cautiously in war and added to the royal treasury by seizing monastic property. Henry and later Elizabeth I moved against England's enemies, the Catholic Church and Spain. Elizabeth made the Church of England officially Protestant and added to her reign the victory over the Spanish Armada.

Farming was the primary occupation for most sixteenth-century Europeans, and small, self-sufficient villages were the main organizational unit in the countryside. Most land was owned by the aristocracy. Sharing common pasture and woodland, peasant families had individual holdings within the village fields. Some peasants paid rents with cash, but most paid in kind or with labor.

Inequality and social stratification governed life in sixteenth-century Europe. Hierarchy was the organizing principle, maintaining orderly relations among widely varying social groups. As the century progressed, urban elites made wealthy by the expanding market economy began challenging the nobility's privileged status.

Multiple-Choice Questions

Choose the best response.

_____ 1. For Philip II, the motivation for sending an armada to invade England was
    a. the desire to aid Catholic rebels in northern England.
    b. the need to establish maritime control of the English Channel.
    c. an attempt to destroy English commerce.
    d. a "holy crusade" against the queen of England.

_____ 2. What country was the greatest power in Europe by the middle of the sixteenth century?
    a. France
    b. Spain
    c. England
    d. Germany

_____ 3. As a Catholic and Christian monarch dedicated to fighting the infidel, Philip II had conflicts with
    a. England.
    b. Portugal.
    c. Greece.
    d. Russia.

_____ 4. The gravest crisis in Philip II's reign was
    a. the war against the Turks.
    b. the revolt of the Netherlands.
    c. conflict with England.
    d. competition with the Portuguese for empire in the New World.

_____ 5. Which of these inflamed passions in France in the 1560s?
    a. Lutheran zeal
    b. Excessive royal power
    c. Economic depression
    d. Aristocratic ambition

_____ 6. French Protestants were called
    a. Anabaptists.
    b. Presbyterians.
    c. Lutherans.
    d. Huguenots.

_____ 7. The massacre of French Protestants in Paris in August 1572 is called
    a. the St. Valentine's Day Massacre.
    b. the St. Bartholomew's Day Massacre.
    c. St. Jerome's Day Massacre.
    d. St. Ignatius Day Massacre.

_____ 8. The act that proclaimed toleration of the Huguenots was
    a. the Ninety-Five Theses.
    b. the Edict of Nantes.
    c. the Edict of Paris.
    d. the Concordat of Worms.

_____ 9. Unlike western Europe, Polish political power rested with the
    a. middle classes.
    b. peasants.
    c. nobles.
    d. Catholic clergy.

_____ 10. Social organization in sixteenth-century Europe was based upon
    a. equality.
    b. stratification.
    c. mobility.
    d. communism.

Answers to Multiple-Choice Questions

1. d	3. a	5. d	7. b	9. c
2. b	4. b	6. d	8. b	10. b

Identification

Briefly identify and summarize the historical significance of each of the following:

the Irish question
Edict of Nantes
Montaigne
Henry IV
Duke of Alba

the Armada
the House of Guise
St. Bartholomew's Day Massacre
Catherine de Medici
Huguenots

Short-Answer and Essay Questions

11. Sixteenth-century Europeans had stronger loyalty to their families and communities than to either church or state. Examine how private life overshadowed such powerful public institutions.

12. Rarely in European history did a country fall from the heights of power as rapidly as Spain did in the decades after 1556. How and why?

13. Define the expressions nation-state, sovereignty, and balance of power, and give an example of each in practice.

14. What were the causes and consequences of the French civil war of 1559 to 1589? Was the conflict chiefly a religious or a political event, or both?

15. Discuss sixteenth-century political theory and how such thought reflected contemporary historical events.

Map Exercise

Map 17.1 **The Spanish Habsburgs and Europe**
Map 17.2 **The Netherlands, 1559–1609**
Map 17.3 **Territories of the Austrian Habsburgs**
Map 17.4 **Two Empires in Eastern Europe ca. 1600**

16. On the outline maps provided, and referring to maps 17.1–17.4, locate and outline the following areas: lands ruled by the Spanish and Austrian Habsburgs, the Ottoman Empire, and the United Provinces (Holland); the boundaries of the Holy Roman Empire by 1600; the expansion of the Russian state or Muscovy from 1300 to 1600. Also mark the Kingdom of Poland circa 1600.

Map 17.1 The Spanish Habsburgs and Europe
Map 17.2 The Netherlands, 1559–1609

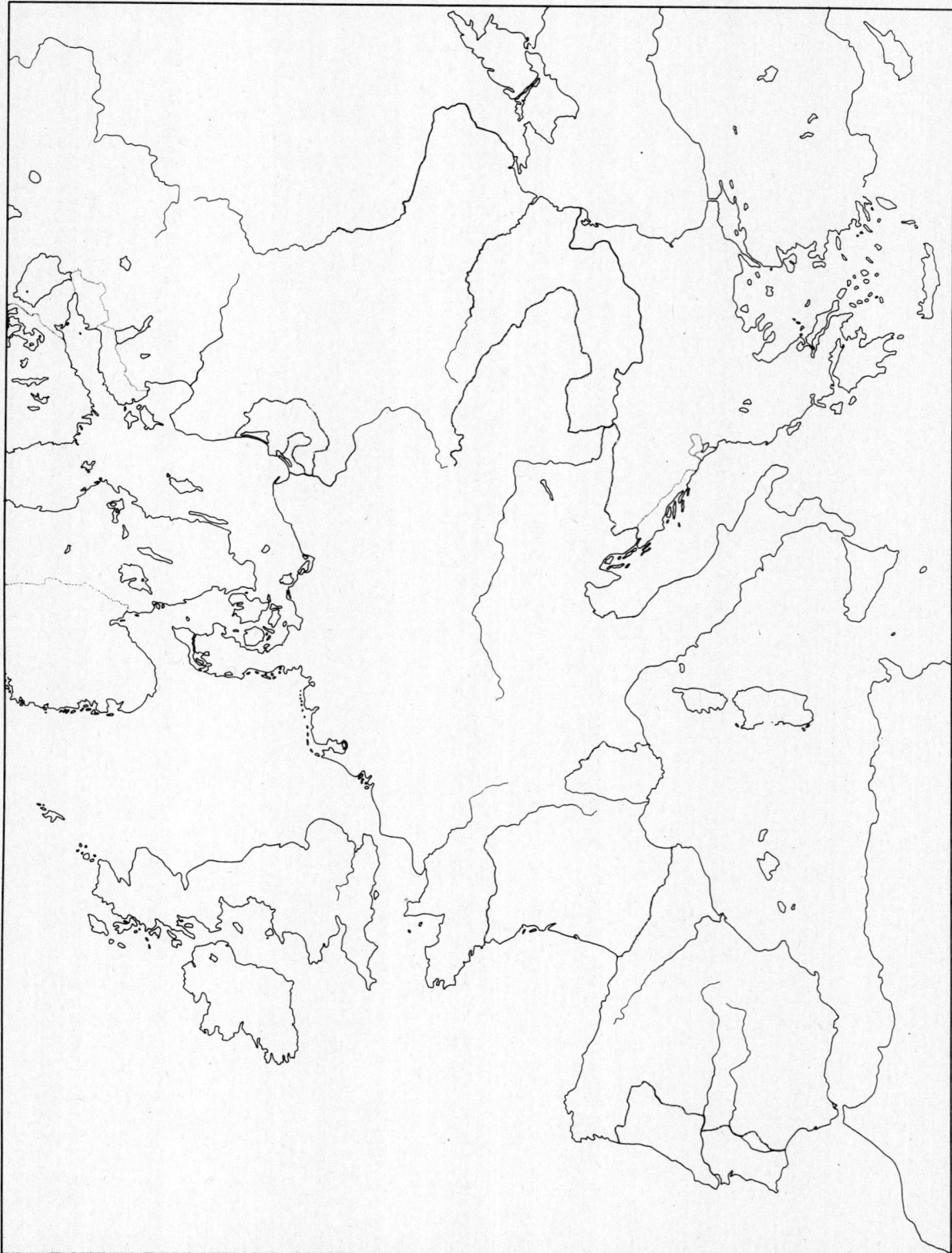

Map 17.3 Territories of the Austrian Habsburgs

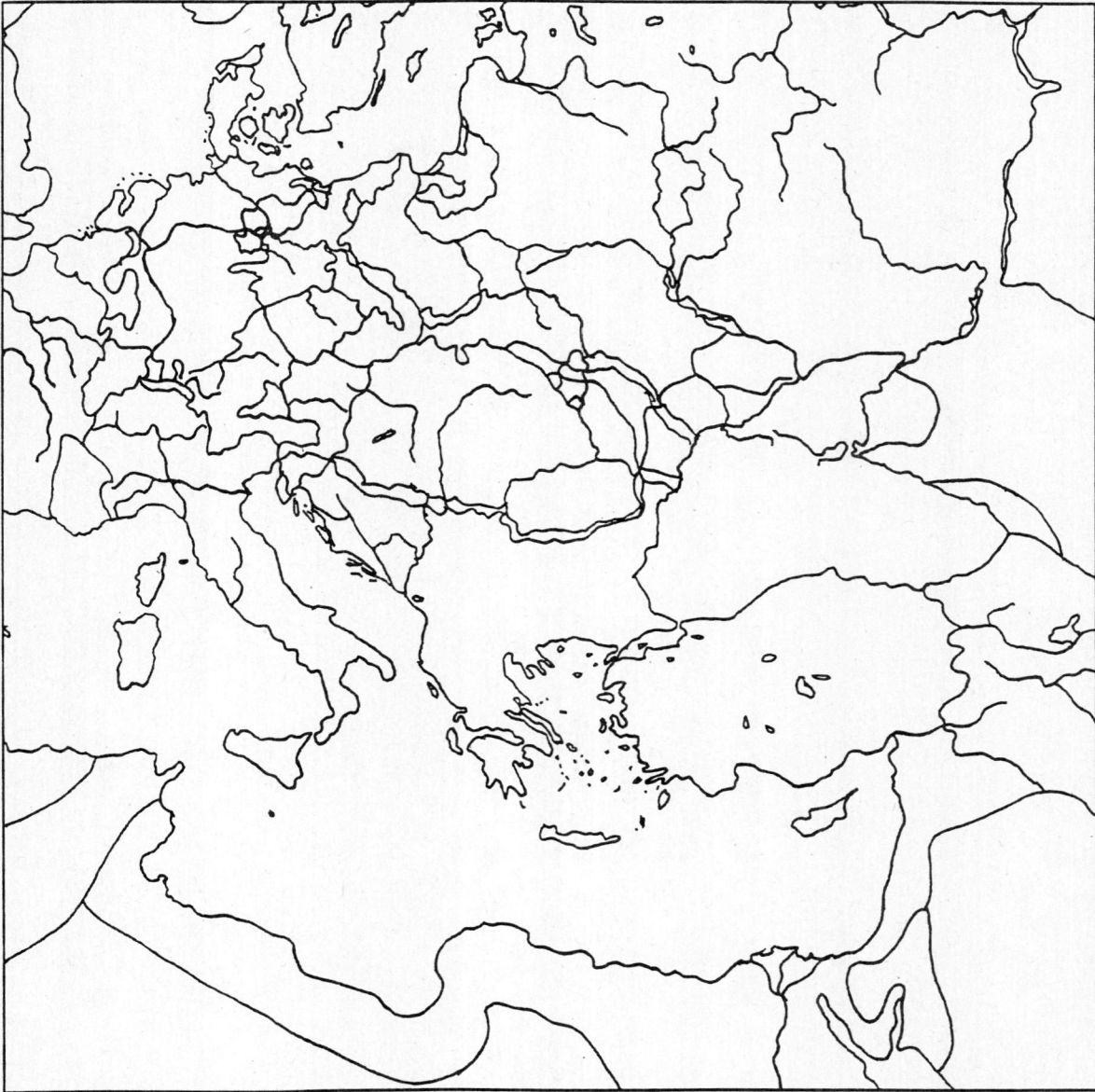

Map 17.4 Two Empires in Eastern Europe ca. 1600

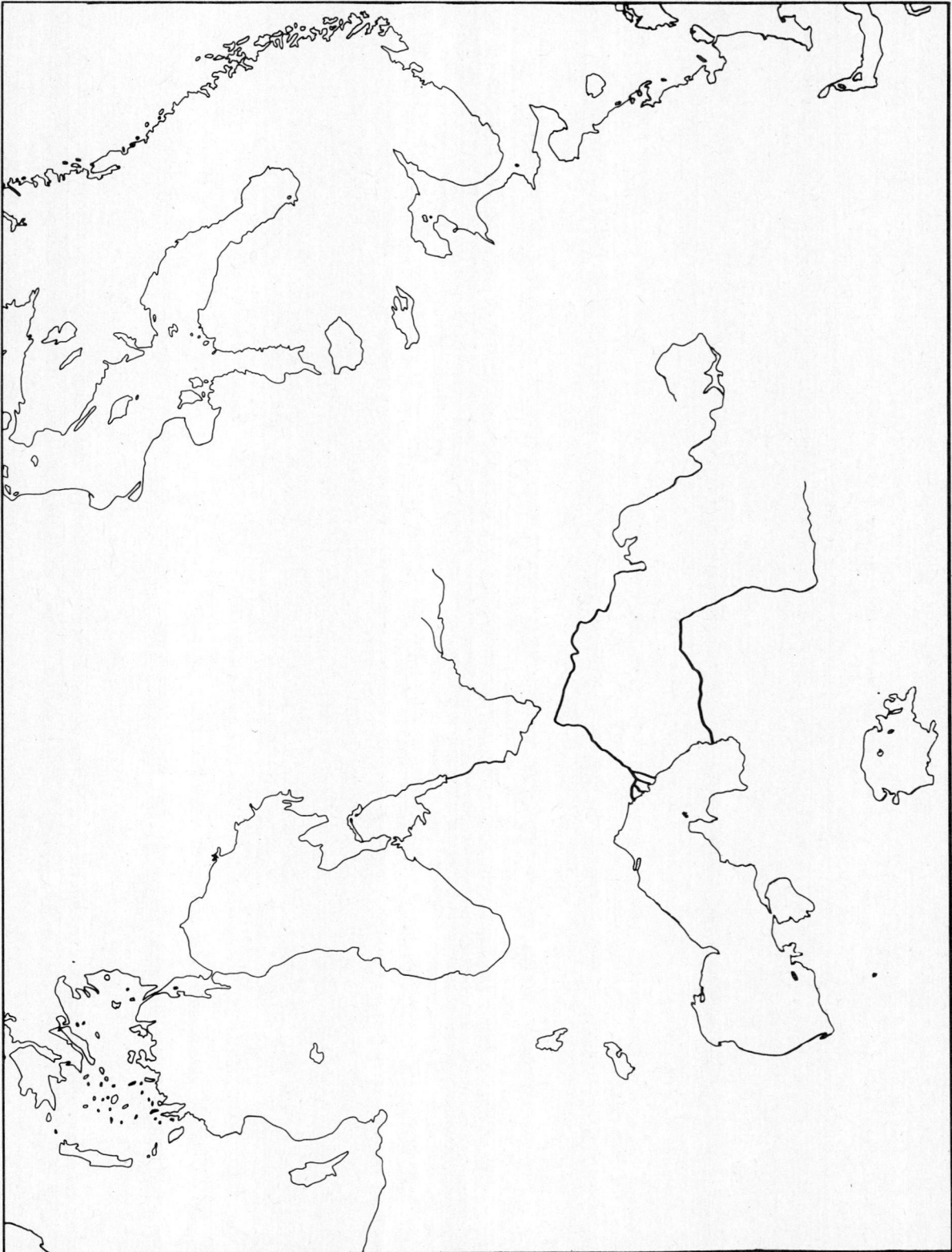

Europe in the Age of Louis XIV, ca. 1610–1715

Learning Objectives

After studying this chapter, you should be able to:

1. understand how absolutism and constitutionalism differed from the feudalism of earlier centuries and cite which countries best represented absolutism and constitutionalism.

2. describe the emergence of absolutism in France under Henry IV and Cardinal Richelieu.

3. explain why Louis XIV can be described as the epitome of the absolute monarch.

4. describe the concept of the monarchy held by the Stuart kings; explain how the English revolution was a response to it, and trace the course of that uprising from 1640 to 1689.

5. understand the economic and geopolitical factors promoting overseas expansion by the English, Dutch, and French in the seventeenth century.

6. explain the rise of Prussia and Russia, noting especially the importance of their monarchs, Frederick William and Peter the Great.

7. explain how traditional society began to change during the sixteenth and seventeenth centuries.

Summary

The Thirty Years' War (1618–1648) began as a religious conflict within the Holy Roman Empire but ended as a political power struggle between France and the Habsburgs. During the war, armies ravaged the countryside, killing not only their enemies but innocent civilians as well. The final settlements, known as the Peace of Westphalia, recognized Calvinism as a tolerated religion, made territorial concessions to France, Sweden, and Brandenburg, and recognized the right of individual German states to conduct their own foreign policies.

By the close of the Thirty Years' War, France had emerged as the most dominant power in Europe. During the reign of Louis XIII and his brilliant minister, Cardinal Richelieu, an efficient, centralized state was established. Richelieu eliminated the Huguenots as a political force, brought the once-proud and autonomous aristocracy under royal control, and made the monarchy absolute in power. Though much credit must be given to Richelieu for making France and its monarchy the most powerful in Europe, it was Louis XIV who made it the most glorious. Few kings have been as successful in establishing complete monarchial sovereignty as the great Sun King.

The mercantilist policies of Colbert, Louis's brilliant minister of finance, expanded foreign trade and industrial expansion. Louis succeeded in expanding France at the expense of the Habsburgs, and his patronage of the arts helped promote the great age of French classicism. However, because of his aggressive foreign policy and the expulsion of the Huguenots, the economic progress of his early reign gave way to contraction and debt.

In England, the Stuart monarchs James I and Charles I violated traditions limiting royal authority and protecting individual rights. Their attempts to rule without Parliament led to civil war (1642–1648). Under Oliver Cromwell, the New Model Army decisively defeated the king's forces. In 1649, Charles was executed for treason.

During the Interregnum, England proclaimed itself a republic, but in reality it was a "benevolent" military dictatorship dominated by Cromwell and the army. Cromwell's regime faced opposition at home and abroad, particularly in Ireland. The English grew weary of Cromwell's righteousness and heavy-handedness, and within a year of his death in 1658 restored the monarchy. But the Interregnum marked the first successful challenge to monarchy by a politicized citizenry. Moreover, the civil war affirmed the existence of an unwritten constitution rooted in English common law. Belief in freedom of speech and religious toleration also emerged in this period.

During the Restoration, Parliament began to assert its power, and Charles II found that it was not possible to stifle it. The openly Catholic sympathies of Charles's successor, James II, further aroused the English people. By 1688, James had so alienated his subjects that Parliament believed it necessary to remove him by force. Bloodshed was avoided as James fled England. Thus, the Glorious Revolution of 1688 was accomplished without violence. Parliament invited William of Orange from Holland to become king and then enacted the Bill of Rights of 1689, embodying the principles of parliamentary supremacy.

The Netherlands emerged by the middle of the seventeenth century as a major European economic and commercial power. Politically Holland was unique in western Europe, developing into a loosely federated, middle-class constitutional state. Spain, however, was the classic case of imperial decline. By 1600, Spain was in trouble, and by the end of the seventeenth century its preeminence was only a memory. Not only did New World bullion and labor run out, but this once-great source of wealth ruined the Spanish economic and social structure. Ongoing conflict with France, England, and Holland also helped to turn Spain into a backwater of Europe.

In central-eastern Europe, Frederick William, the Great Elector of Brandenburg-Prussia, employed absolutist rule with great success. By the 1660s, Frederick had not only consolidated his holdings into a well-managed centralized state but had also built a disciplined army. The consolidation of the Russian state followed a similar path. Peter I (Peter the Great), enamored of western military techniques and government structure, introduced conscription to create a standing army in which promotion was based on merit, and the Russians gradually emerged as the dominant Baltic power.

In the seventeenth century, England established permanent colonies in North America, overrunning earlier Dutch and Swedish settlements. Unlike the Spanish and French colonies, where royal governors represented centralized bureaucracies, English royal governors lacked extensive authority.

In the St. Lawrence region, the French established New France. The search for fur led to exploration of the North American interior, but only a few Frenchmen were willing to establish permanent colonial settlements in the Mississippi valley.

Both the Spanish-held West Indies—where sugar, tobacco, fruit, and coffee crops were profitable exports—and the East Indies became battlegrounds for imperialist powers. At the same time western European nations expanded overseas, Russia explored and conquered a vast Asian empire that stretched across Siberia to the Pacific. The age of European expansion resulted in the horrors of the slave trade, the extermination of native populations, and the undermining of social arrangements that had existed for centuries. Expansion revolutionized western European economies and societies. As Portugal, Spain, France, Holland, and England explored and conquered the New World, they set the stage for international politics for centuries to come.

Multiple-Choice Questions

Choose the best response.

_____ 1. All of the following were factors in the Thirty Years' War *except*
  a. the religious struggle of Catholics against Protestants.
  b. the dynastic struggle between the Habsburgs and their enemies.
  c. the Bohemian revolt against a Habsburg king.
  d. the conflict between Spain and the Holy Roman Empire over possessions in Italy.

_____ 2. The policies of Cardinal Richelieu rested on the idea that
  a. the participation of the aristocracy in the bureaucracy would lead to monarchial support.
  b. above all, reasons of state must be served.
  c. toleration of Huguenots would unite all of France.
  d. the feudal ideal of a Christian commonwealth of nations must be restored.

_____ 3. Richelieu's policies included all of the following *except*
  a. active support for Protestant forces against the Habsburgs during the Thirty Years' War.
  b. a general act of religious toleration in France.
  c. war against Spain.
  d. limiting Huguenot influence in France.

_____ 4. At the center of the developing nation-states in seventeenth-century western Europe were
  a. the hierarchy and bureaucracy of the Roman Catholic church.
  b. the king and his court.
  c. powerful commercial bankers.
  d. powerful feudal aristocrats.

_____ 5. Which of the following statements *best* characterizes seventeenth-century monarchs?
  a. They were essentially the same as twentieth-century dictators, exercising total control over the life and death of their subjects.
  b. They were larger-than-life personalities, adept at assuming whatever role the state demanded of them.
  c. At best they were efficient facilitators and royal overseers; at worst they were inefficient, reclusive, and negligent leaders.
  d. They were only figureheads, and real power rested with a resurgent Catholic church and the aristocracy.

_____ 6. England was not a likely candidate for a direct challenge to monarchial authority for all of the following reasons *except*
  a. its strength had not been sapped by the Thirty Years' War.
  b. England alone had enjoyed peace in the early seventeenth century.
  c. taxation had remained relatively light.
  d. a good working rapport existed between the Stuarts and the English gentry.

_____ 7. The crisis that caused Charles I to summon Parliament in 1640 and that helped precipitate the English civil war was
  a. the successful invasion of England by a Scottish army.
  b. the king's need to live off of the nation's revenues.
  c. the fear that the king's ministers were conspiring against the Crown.
  d. the invasion of French forces.

_____ 8. The document that reasserted the fundamental rights of security of property, the regularity of Parliaments, and religious toleration for all Protestants was the
  a. Magna Carta.
  b. Constitution of Clarendon.
  c. Declaration of Rights.
  d. English Constitution.

_____ 9. One of the major causes of war in the middle to late seventeenth century was
  a. military ambition.
  b. national honor.
  c. commercial advantage.
  d. dynastic rivalry.

Answers to Multiple-Choice Questions

1. d	3. b	5. c	7. a	9. c
2. b	4. b	6. d	8. c	

Identification

Briefly identify and summarize the historical significance of each of the following:

Frederick William   Cardinal Richelieu
Edict of Nantes   Thirty Years' War
Peter the Great   New Model Army
Glorious Revolution   absolutism
Oliver Cromwell   Louis XIV

Short-Answer and Essay Questions

10. Discuss the causes of the English revolutions of 1640 and 1689.

11. Describe the achievements and failures of Louis XIV.

12. Discuss the major causes, history, and consequences of the Thirty Years' War.

13. Discuss the various economic and geopolitical factors that gave rise to the commercial revolution of the seventeenth century.

14. Compare and contrast the political evolution of France and England in the seventeenth century. Of the two states, which developed a more "modern" polity?

Map Exercises

Map 18.1 Europe in the Thirty Years' War

15. On the outline map provided, show the boundaries of the Austrian Habsburg empire, the Spanish Habsburg empire, the Prussian empire, the Swedish empire, and the German states that became independent of the Holy Roman Empire.

Map 18.3 New Powers in Central and Eastern Europe

16. On the outline map provided, show the boundaries of the Russian empire under Peter the Great and show the Prussian expansion from 1640 to 1748. What happened to Poland?

Map 18.4 Dutch Commerce in the Seventeenth Century

17. On the outline map provided, indicate the European territory acquired by England, France, and Holland in the seventeenth century.

Map 18.5 British and French in North America ca. 1700

18. On the outline map provided, label the New World territory acquired by England, France, and Spain.

Map 18.1 Europe in the Thirty Years' War

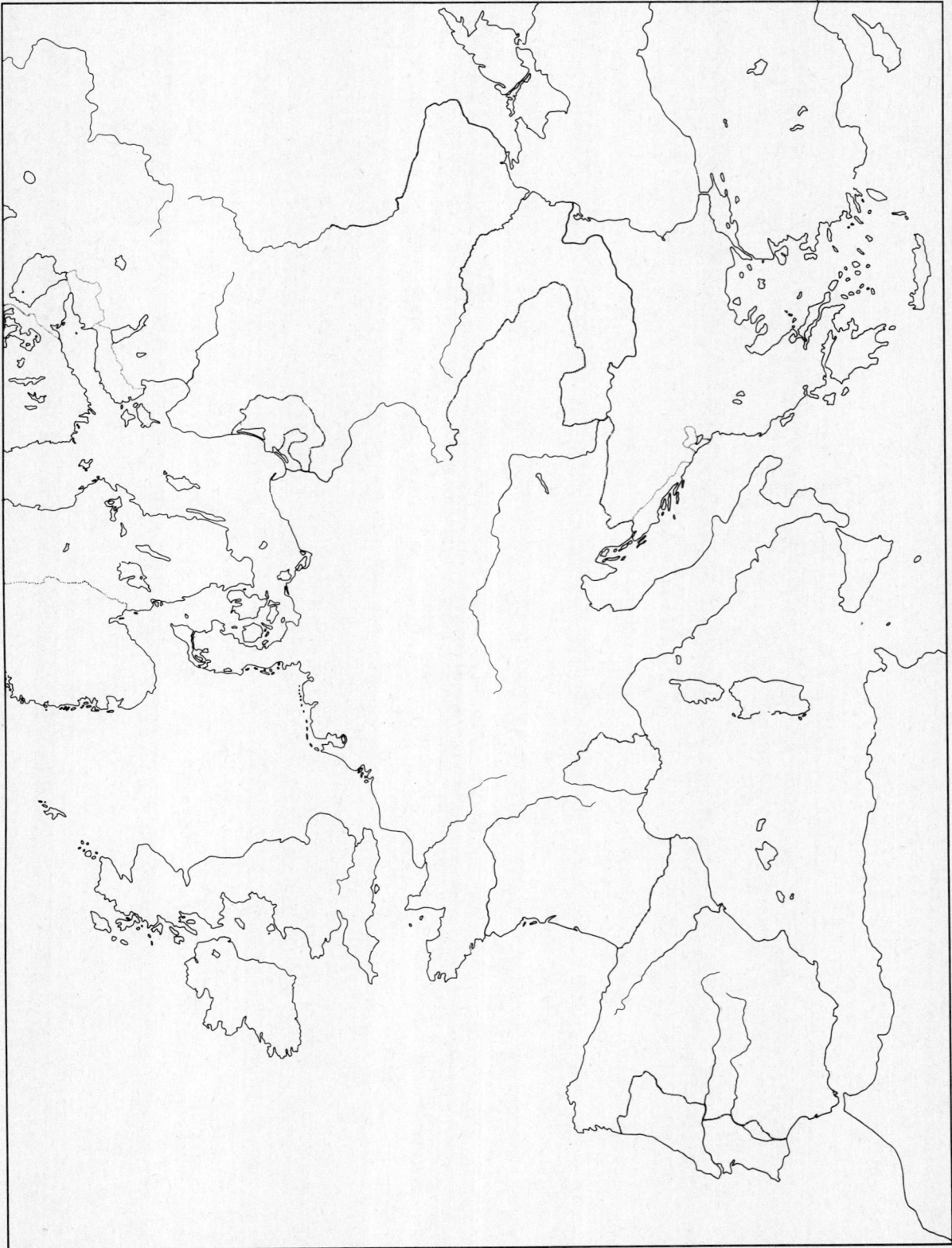

Map 18.3 New Powers in Central and Eastern Europe

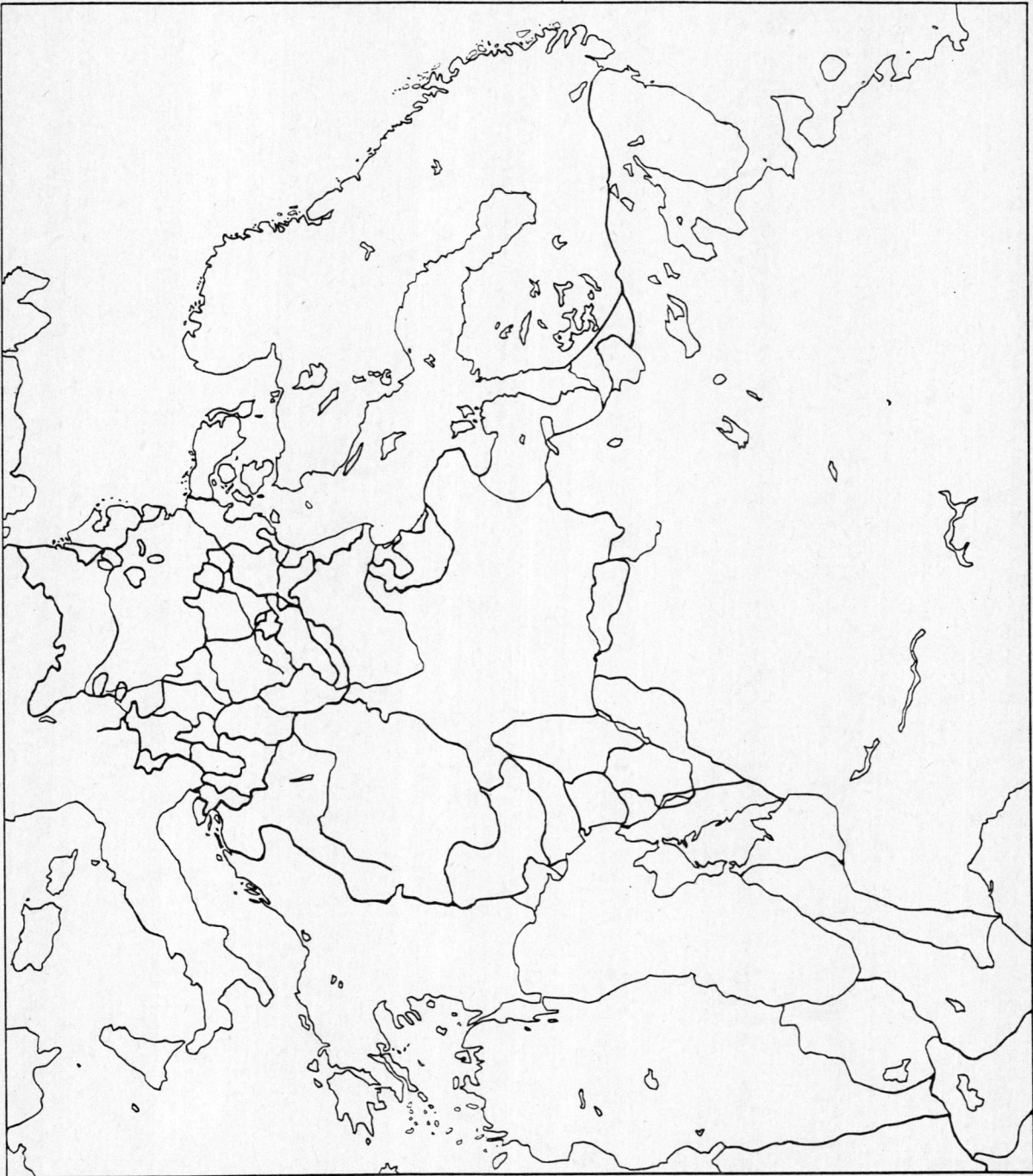

Map 18.4 Dutch Commerce in the Seventeenth Century

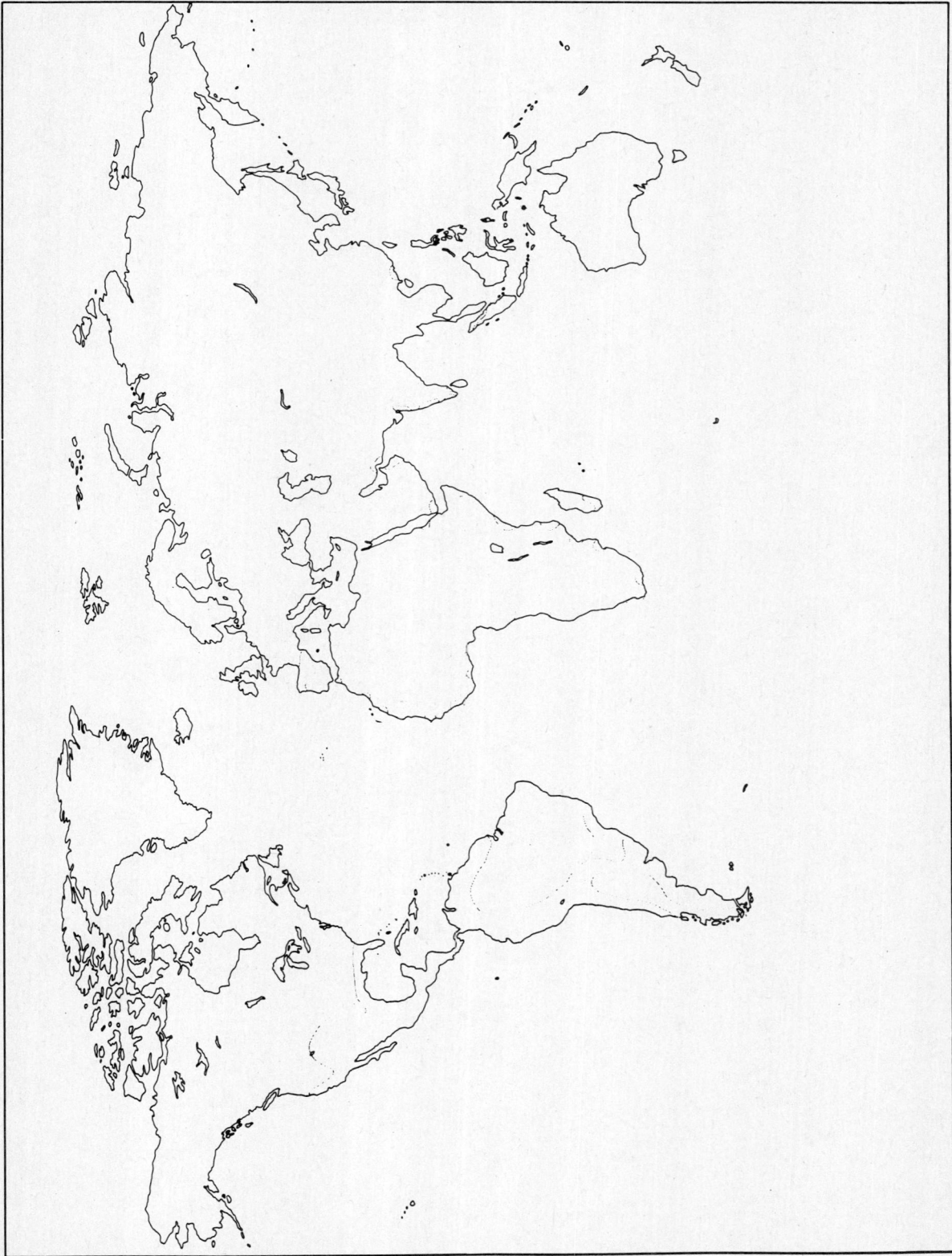

Map 18.5 British and French in North America ca. 1700

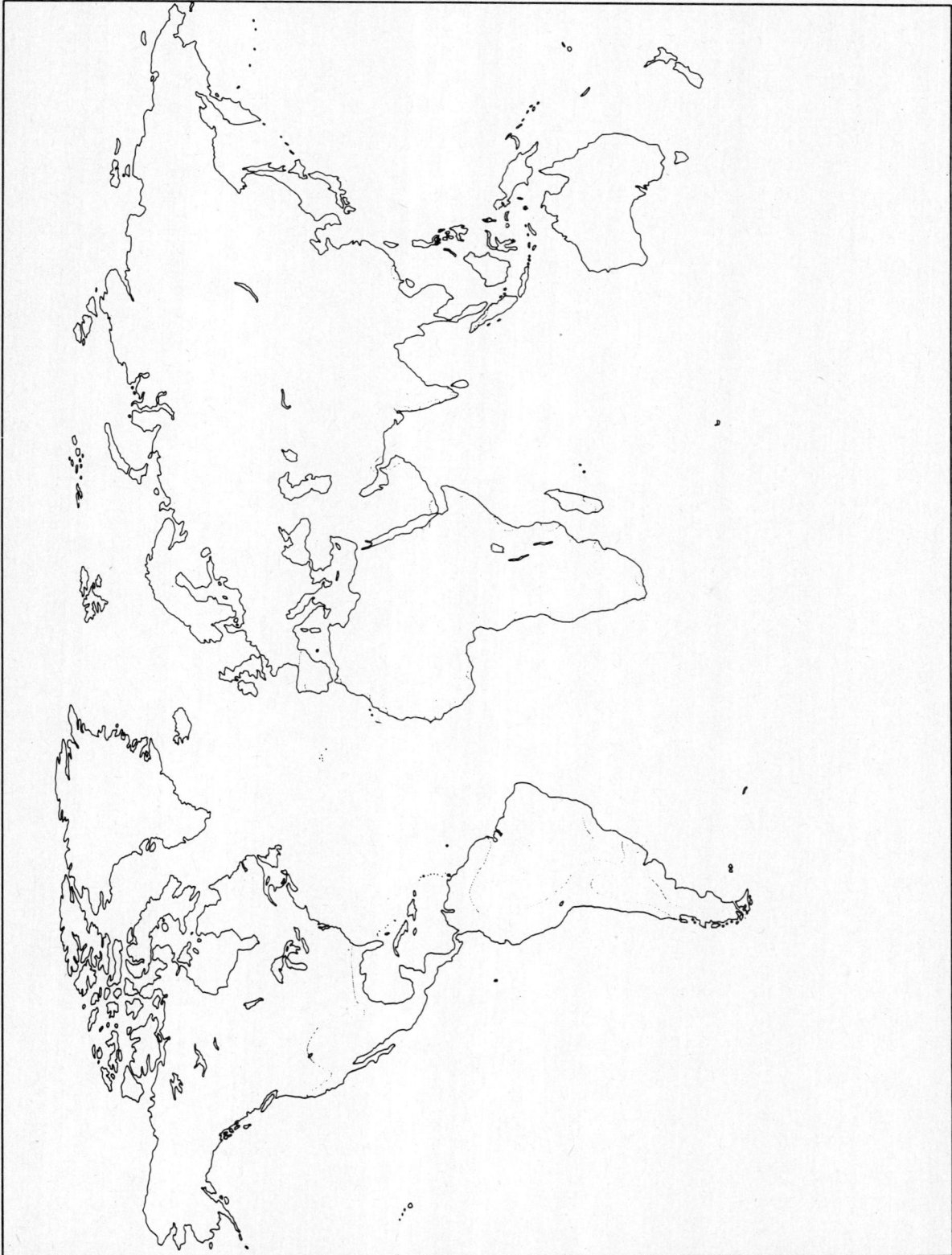

Chapter 1
The Ancestors of the West

11. Answers should include discussing the signs of modern human culture; forming of villages; domestication of plants and animals; development of Neolithic towns.

12. Answers should include discussing the importance of Ugarit to the resurgence of urban life in Syria; its cosmopolitanism; its role as a center of trade.

13. Answers should include discussing queens' and queen mothers' strong and independent positions in Hittite society; their influence in religious affairs.

14. Answers should include discussing the role of war in the international system; the importance of treaties; the collapse of Mesopotamian, Greek, Anatolian, and Egyptian states between 1250 and 1150 B.C.

15. Answers should include Mesopotamia and Egypt becoming complex societies; their social, economic, and class hierarchies; the role of religion in each society; their political institutions; their architecture; their technological advances; their writing; their art and culture; their settled agriculture; their influence on the Hittite, Syro-Palestine, and Greek civilizations.

Chapter 2
The Book and the Myths: Western Asia and Early Greece

11. Answers should include discussing the Hebrew Bible as the first national history book; its covenant and its semidivine foundations; the meaning given to history by the covenant with God; the Torah, the Prophets, and the Scriptures; Homer's *Iliad* and *Odyssey*; the polytheistic gods; their human characteristics and foibles; their comparative power, immediacy, and interest in the inner lives of human beings compared to Yahweh.

12. Answers should include discussing the role of Phoenicians in spreading literacy and urbanism to both sides of the Mediterranean; their technological advances in shipbuilding; their travel to Africa, the British Isles, and, possibly Brazil, as well as within the Mediterranean region; their role as middlemen in the trading world of the Mediterranean and the inland civilizations.

13. Answers should include understanding that the Hebrews were originally polytheistic; the patriarchs' role in the move toward monotheism; the effect of the Exodus on the move toward monotheism; the role of Moses; the relationship of man to God that was an important part of developing monotheism; the influence of the Israelite kings.

14. Answers should include discussing the Persian concept, the "King of Kings"; characteristics of the kings; kings' displays of royal authority.

15. Answers should include briefly summarizing achievements in metallurgy and imperialism in the first half of the first millennium B.C.; growing importance of attempting to understand the meaning of human life; Hebrew civilizations' evolution toward monotheism; the Persians' development of Zoroastrianism; attempts by Greek writers like Homer and Hesiod to understand human nature and humans' relationship to the world; societies into which these changes came; the reasons for their coming; results of attempts to understand the meaning of human existence in each civilization studied.

Chapter 3
The Age of the Polis: Greece, ca. 750–370 B.C.

11. Answers should include discussing Sparta's history as a military society; its lack of trust and contempt for book learning; its feelings toward foreigners; its attempts to keep its affairs private; its three-part class system; its diet; its belief in *agoge*.

12. Answers should include discussing the Olympian gods' role as the gods of the polis; the patron gods' role for each polis; building temples to honor the gods in each polis; specific examples of gods and the polei they reigned over.

13. Answers should include discussing the Sophists, their respect for success; importance of rhetoric; Hippocrates; Socrates and his role as a teacher; the Ionian natural-philosophy tradition; Plato, Aristotle, and their respective philosophies and approaches to philosophy.

14. Answers should include Athens' move from tyranny to democracy; revolution led by Cleisthenes; role of the *demos*; division of Athenians into ten tribes; role of the assembly; effect of the foreign-affairs setback in the fifth century; role of Pericles.

15. Answers should include discussing the polis becoming an important institution in the Greek city-states; the ways in which the polis came to denote the community as a whole in the Greek world; the two parts of the polis; physical structure of the polis; role of the hoplite phalanx in the polis; role of *arete*; tyranny in the polis; role of tyrants in developing the Greek city-states.

Chapter 4
The Hellenistic World

11. Answers should include identifying Macedon, Ptolemaic Egypt, and the Seleucid kingdom; Macedon as a border state with rich resources and manpower; its lack of efficient political organization; its language and social organization; its army; its federal leagues; Ptolemaic Egypt as the wealthiest and most sophisticated of the Hellenistic kingdoms; its language; its monarchs; its marriage practices; its glory in wealth and grandeur; tradition of command economy combined with customs of literacy and monetary economy; the Seleucid kingdom's

domination by a Greek-speaking elite; its far-flung and multiethnic character; its system of satraps, taxes, royal roads, and post; its excellent army.

12. Answers should include comparing the raucous Old Comedy with the restrained New Comedy; focus on war and politics in Old Comedy; domestic and private focus in New Comedy; New Comedy of Menander; role of critics in Alexandria; preference for short poems in the Hellenistic world, especially in the work of Callimachus.

13. Answers should include discussing the split between science and medicine in the Hellenistic world; Antigonid patronage of ethical and political philosophy; Alexandrian study of science; the work of Euclid, Apollonius of Perge, Archimedes of Syracuse, Aristarchus of Samos, Hipparchus of Nicaea, Eratosthenes of Cyrene, Herophilus of Chalcedon, and Erasistratus of Ceos.

14. Answers should include discussing the little contact Greeks and Jews had before Alexander's conquests; Greek government of Judea; Jewish independence movement; relationship of fascination and hatred, assimilation and violence, conversion and apostasy between the two groups; role of the Ptolemies; establishing Greek colonies in and around Judea; abandoning some members of the Jewish elite for the Greek gymnasium; resistance by the traditionalists; the Jewish diaspora; the guerrilla movement; development of a Jewish literature; acceptance of the redeemer concept in this era; use of Greek as the common language in the diaspora; development of anti-Semitic literature.

15. Answers should include yielding of Greek hegemony to Macedon in the fourth century B.C.; role of Philip and Alexander in Macedon's conquests; colonialism of the Macedonians; their rule in Egypt and western Asia; new cities built with the new Greek wealth; increase and expansion of trade; expansion of political life; importance of the Federal Leagues; cultural changes including the new philosophies of the Stoics, Cynics, Epicureans, and Skeptics; new religions, including the mystery religions; Hellenistic Judaism; advances in science and medicine; changing role of the individual in art and society.

Chapter 5
The Rise of the Roman Republic

11. Answers should include development of economic empire; Punic Wars; assimilation and relatively good treatment of conquered peoples.

12. Answers should include Etruscan engineering accomplishments; architecture; funerary practices and belief in life after death; funeral games; artistic skills like fresco painting; divination; urbanizing the city of Rome; artisanship and commerce; military power.

13. Answers should include defining *paterfamilias*; his relationship to the rest of the family; his supreme power under Roman law; his right to sell family members into slavery; his relationship to his sons; his property rights; his representation of the family to divine and human outside authority; his regular performance of sacrifices; the reciprocal relationship inherent in the role of paterfamilias; his relationship to his wife and daughters.

14. Answers should include defining *patron* and *client*; the pyramidal structure of the patron–client system; importance of mutual respect; paths that led to the status of client; examples of ways in which patrons and clients helped each other; importance of *fides* to the relationship; solemnity of the relationship between patrons and clients; effect of the patron–client relationship on the political process in Rome; extending the relationship to conquered lands.

15. Answers should include discussing the flexibility and stability of the Republic's oligarchy; accommodating the aristocracy's competitive instincts and the Romans' land hunger; developing the hierarchy and including some wealthy members of the plebs; efforts by the elites to protect Rome from its enemies in central Italy; Rome's consolidating its control over central Italy; extending Roman citizenship; Roman quest for absolute security; the influence of greed and ambition on the expanding Republic; effects of contact with the Greeks; influx of slaves to the Republic; weakening of the peasants; increasing arogance of the patricians; confiscation of peasant lands.

Chapter 6
Roman Revolution and Imperial Rome, 133 B.C.–A.D. 284

11. Answers should include discussing Cicero's intelligence, ambition, and literary talents; his work as an orator, essayist, letter writer, lawyer, and politician; his effect on development of Roman law.

12. Answers should include and identify both Virgil and Horace; Virgil's role as spokesperson of his age; grandeur of his themes; emotion with which he wrote; Horace's polished, complex, less emotional work; themes of war and peace; his praise for Augustus; both of the men's successful adaptation of Greek models; they created something new.

13. Answers should include discussing irony, satire, pithiness, formality, and rhetorical flourish of writing in the Silver Age; compilation of handbooks and encyclopedias, self-consciousness and literary criticism; geographical diversity of the writers' backgrounds; pursuit of public careers by many writers; influence of writers like Tacitus, Juvenal, Plutarch, Matthew, Mark, Luke, and John.

14. Answers should include Jesus of Nazareth's themes of praise for the poor and humble, scorn for the pursuit of wealth instead of righteousness; his call for generosity and forgiveness; his emphasis that prayer, fasting, and charity should be practiced in private to ensure purity of motive; his views on sex and divorce.

15. Answers should include discussing Octavian's rise to power; his use of the title *princeps*; his partnership with the senate; his dispersing administrative authority to appease various groups and to foster efficient government; his distinction from his predecessors; his creating the first civil service for Rome, Italy, and the provinces; affluence of the era; his reforms in the military; his accepting Germans on the frontier; his creating client kingdoms; a more effective method of distributing grain; his sponsoring social legislation that espoused old Republican virtues; continued professionalizing of Roman law; your opinion on whether these reforms were beneficial or ultimately detrimental to Rome.

Chapter 7
The World of Late Antiquity, ca. 300–600

11. Answers should include discussing Valentinian's decision to appoint his two sons to military commands; their troops' insistence that the two be named *augusti*; the military's interest in imperial leaders and patrons of their own; Valens's death in battle; the appointment and rise of Theodocious I who became the most powerful man in the Roman world.

12. Answers should include discussing attempts by Diocletian, Constantine, Constantius II, Julian, and Gratian to promote unity; problem of trying to unify a large population; diversity of the Roman population; power struggle among the elite; struggle between Christianity and paganism.

13. Answers should include discussing turnover of the aristocratic class in Roman society; opportunities for social mobility; including provincial ruling classes and Germans in the framework of power and influence in Rome; continuity within the change.

14. Answers should include discussing change over the years from Germans living on the frontiers of the empire and serving as auxiliary troops to their move across the frontier; understanding similarities and differences of the Huns, Visogoths, Ostrogoths; local authorities' exploiting the Germans; increasing presence of Germans in the Roman army; Visigothic sack of Rome and their treaty with Rome.

15. Answers should include discussing administrative, political, economic, and military reforms of the various emperors; assimilation of Germans into the Roman Empire; legalization and rise of Christianity; continuation of the classical order of hierarchy; continued flowering of Roman culture, albeit different from that of classical antiquity.

Chapter 8
Early Medieval Civilizations, ca. 600–900

11. Answers should include discussing size and turbulence of the Arab world early in the seventh century; predominance of clans and tribes in Arab society; diversity of the region's ethnic and religious groups; influence of the Bedouins; support of traders in the cities; competition among tribes; development of harems.

12. Answers should include discussing succession of caliphs; expansion of the caliphate; use of the *jihad* to expand Islam; careful planning by the Muslin conquests to channel violence out of Arabia.

13. Answers should include discussing Leo III's victories against the Muslims and Bulgars; his military reforms; his issuance of the Ecloga; his and Constantine's reforms of imperial administration; promotion of religious and cultural unity; personal convictions of the rulers; death of Leo IV and rise of Irene's regency for her son; Constantine IV's frivolity; Irene's rule of the empire; shifts in religious policy; a series of assassinations and usurpations; some military defeats; shortage of state cash; coup d'état that brought Irene's reign to an end.

14. Answers should include discussing the three processes that led to the development of the papal state; decline of Roman imperial power; role of popes in protecting the people of central Italy; creating a justification for papal temporal rule; the *Donation of Constantine*; dual role of medieval popes as head of church and state; Gregory I.

15. Answers should include discussing the trade and commerce practices of the Byzantine empire; role of leadership in defending the empire; relatively smaller geographic area the empire had to defend; common sense of danger to the empire that proved helpful in unifying it for defense; tradition and history of the empire.

Chapter 9
The Frontiers of the Latin West, ca. 600–1300

11. Answers should include discussing physical differences in each of the Celtic lands and how that affected development; fertile land of Ireland; five provinces of Ireland; harsh weather of Wales; its small population; its contacts with the other Celtic realms by sea; heterogeneousness of Scottish society; physical diversity of the Scottish geography; powerful, ambitious individuals in each of the Celtic lands; development of the church as an important institution; influence of the Vikings.

12. Answers should include discussing the Moravians, Czechs, and Slovaks; the Magyars; the Russians; their domination at times be foreign powers; ethnic diversity; their lack of loyalty to reigning dynasties; their conversion to Christianity; lack of bonds strong enough to overcome old tensions; independent aristocratic power; autonomous towns.

13. Answers should include discussing the role of political, commercial, and military external controls; slow forming of centralized states; insignificance of Latin culture and abundance of Old Norse literature.

14. Answers should include discussing breakdown of the caliphate into three major areas; their further split into smaller entities; military threats; religious strife that helped loosen bonds of loyalty; cycle of political disruption, economic decline, and political struggle that further broke down the Islamic state.

15. Answers should include discussing frontiers of the Latin West: Celtic lands, Scandinavia, Slavic world, Byzantium, and Islamic state; diversity of experience within those lands; geographic diversity and range; difficulty in creating centralized governments in places; influence of religion as a unifying and divisive influence; importance of art and architecture and intellectual achievements of the Islamic state; diversity of political ideas; competing trade interests of the "West."

Chapter 10
The Expansion of Europe, ca. 900–1150

11. Answers should include discussing family size; mortality rate; life expectancy; dangers of childbirth; lack of significant plague between 780 and 1345; no catastrophic incidents of lack and hunger; relatively insignificant crime; new land brought into cultivation.

12. Answers should include discussing traditional order of society: nobles, clergy, and peasants; feeling of nobles and clergy that they were superior to workers; struggles for leadership between nobles and clergy; their dependence on the peasants for subsistence; reciprocity of the relationships; failure to include townspeople and non-Christians; relatively closed orders of society; role of women within orders of society; differences between monastic clergy and episcopal clergy.

13. Answers should include discussing persistence of some traditional roles; women's roles in the church; some participation, however limited, in the military; mistresses of castles; local political powers; chivalry changes this arrangement; women no longer allowed to ride to arms; consolidation of lineages by aristocratic families; less freedom in the marriage market; lack of independent rights over land.

14. Answers should include a brief summary of society's traditional structure: the tripartite model; development of feudal system; importance of castles; free persons who turned over

their properties to local lords and received them back in return for rents or personal services; dependent status of some formerly free persons; reciprocal economic bonds between lords and peasants; personal and public bonds; structure of individual manors; increasing prosperity of peasants in the eleventh and twelfth centuries and reaction of the lords.

15. Answers should include discussing the two sides of the controversy over lay investiture; Henry IV's desire to restore royal power; Gregory VII's interest in papal power and unease with power of lay people within the church; battle of wills between Henry IV and Gregory VII; its influence on Henry; on Gregory; the Concordat of Worms.

Chapter 11
Medieval Civilization at Its Height, ca. 1150–1300

11. Answers should include discussing James I of Aragon, Ferdinand III, and Alfonso X of Castile; their piety; their feelings about the Crusade; their promotion of the church; their style of rule; their individual accomplishments.

12. Answers should include discussing reorganization of the European urban population; cities as centers for activities, including governments and trade; urban-based ecclesiastical organizations; growing wealth; the guilds.

13. Answers should include discussing the *Comedy* as a long and difficult poem; its humor, instruction, and emotion; its Italian language; its base of advanced theology and philosophy; its blend of poetic traditions and common sense; its allegorical journey of the human race; its primary metaphor, love.

14. Answers should include discussing Frederick Barbarossa, Henry VI, Louis VII, and Philip Augustus; ambition of the German kings to restore centralized power; their interest, or lack thereof, in Italy; their conflicts with the pope; the French kings' steadily growing power; growth of French royal revenues; their continuation of Capetian policies.

15. Answers should include discussing the Bull *Clericis laicos*; response to bull of Philip of France; Boniface III's counterresponse; bull *Esti de statu*; effect of Philip's edict on Rome; Boniface's characteristics and alliances as pope; canonization of Louis IX; Boniface's role in attempts to heal the rift between England and France; Boniface's vision of a Christian Europe; Philip IV's 1301 trial of a French bishop; the bull *Ausculta, fili carissime*; Boniface's reaction to the trial; Philip's counterreaction; the bull *Unam Sanctam*; Philip's response to the bull; Boniface's fate.

Chapter 12
The Late Medieval Crisis in Government and Society

11. Answers should include discussing inability of any monarch to claim absolute power; financial constraints and legal theories that prevented absolute power; natural advisers to kings; military operations that depended on money; kings' ability to tax; role of Parliaments; relationship between monarchs and aristocracies of Europe; monarchs' relationship with the provinces; slow development of nationalism.

12. Answers should include discussing the first phase in the war (1337–1360); English *chevau-chées*; Crown Prince Edward; English victories; characteristics of the French knights; weapons used; Battle of Crécy; negotiation; the second phase (1360–1396); French victories that led to recovery of land they lost in the first phase; Richard II; expense of the phase; the third phase (1396–1422); French resistance; Charles VI; Henry V; Agincourt; deaths of Charles and Henry; the fourth phase (1422–1453); French reconquest; Joan of Arc; cessation of hostilities.

13. Answers should include discussing bubonic plague; triangular trade of Italy, Flanders, and North Africa; Italy as the center of European trade; collapse of Italy's financial houses; prosperity tied to agriculture; Statue of Laborers; role of women in European economies; role of guilds.

14. Answers should include discussing the role of trade in the Black Death; bacillus responsible for the plague; Europe's mortality rates; quarantines and embargoes resulting from contagiousness of plague; explanations for plague; reactions to those explanations; the second pestilence; economic changes; stagnant population levels.

15. Answers should include discussing the Hundred Years' War; the Bubonic Plague; the Great Schism; increasing cost of government; monarchs who found it difficult to deal with problems of the fourteenth century; subsistence crisis; relationship between monarchs and their provinces; popular revolts and heresies; promise of the fifteenth century.

Chapter 13
The Late Medieval Recovery

11. Answers should include discussing shifts in patterns of trade and manufacturing in Europe; development of new trade networks; the de' Medicis; Hanseatic League; lower rents and increased wages for small farmers and laborers; increased consumption of meat and fish; increased emphasis on grain farming; transformation of crafts and industry; cloth production.

12. Answers should include discussing dramatic changes in economy of cloth manufacture; the move of urban workshops to countryside; role of the guilds; controls on quality and techniques; the putting-out system; part-time labor; role of merchants; roles of Spain and England, Flanders and Italy.

13. Answers should include discussing religious houses for women; the general public's belief that well-run communities of women added to the community's spiritual and physical health; appeal of the religious communities to women and their families; convents as economical, safe, controlled environments for women; Margery Kempe; the Beguines.

14. Answers should include discussing fear of royal power in England; fear of increased taxation; ascension to the throne by the Lancastrians; Henry VI; loss of most French territories by the English in 1453; house of York; Edward VI and his sons; Richard III; Henry VII; success of the Tudors.

15. Answers should include discussing decrease in threat of the plague, wars, and economic dislocation; lowered rents and higher wages for agricultural workers; change in agricultural production and consumption; change in patterns of commercial trade; importance of a more complex economic life; reform of the church; religious brotherhoods; women's religious communities; development of a new papal administrative structure; the church's cultural and ideological programs; popes' new explanations of religious authority; strengthening of local, regional, and national governments; rise of Spain and the Ottoman Turks.

Chapter 14
The Renaissance

11. Answers should include discussing relative wealth and power of the Gonzaga; Gianfrancesco; Lodovico; creating a brilliant court; artists who frequented the court; importance of Humanism; role of the school; "La Giocosa"; patronage of art with classical themes; importance of the church.

12. Answers should include discussing *The Book of the Courtier*; importance of the courts in Castiglione's works; great changes in late medieval chivalry; importance of Greek classics; his beliefs in quality of "grace"; his beliefs about good and evil; Rabelais's promotion of sensual pleasures.

13. Answers should include discussing Christian Humanism; its Italian origin; its peak outside of Italy; importance of the reform of Christianity; intensive efforts to remove errors from Christian documents; variety of ideas within the movement.

14. Answers should include discussing the importance of classical art and literature to the Renaissance; Roman influence on the Italian Renaissance.

15. Answers should include discussing influence of the courts; patronage; exploration; rise of nation-states; recovery of Italy from the Black Death earlier than the rest of Europe; role of universities; prosperity of Italy; role of the church; individual brilliance of the "Renaissance Man"; quest for public acclaim in artistic or intellectual pursuits, business, administration, construction, entertaining, hunting, and warfare; Leonardo da Vinci; Michelangelo; the Court of Mantua.

Chapter 15
Europe, the Old World and the New

11. Answers should include the important inventions and breakthroughs in maritime technology, such as the astrolabe and better cartography, as well as European desire for access to spice trade of the Orient, dominated by Arabs and Italians; (Venetians).

12. Answers should focus on European military and technological superiority and "disease factor," which contributed more to death of Native Americans than enslavement or slaughter. Europeans had few compunctions about enslaving non-Europeans, especially Native Americans, and slaughtered entire villages for plunder. Also mention that Europeans regarded people of color or non-Europeans as inferior in both race and religion, often adding to their zeal for conquest and wealth, especially Spanish conquistadores.

13. Answers should include Hernán Cortés: conqueror of the great Aztec civilization; representative of the warrior mentality of Spanish conquistadores—a product of the Spanish Reconquista, and the one most responsible for opening up to Spain and other Europeans potential wealth of the mainland in both North and South America. *De Las Casas:* a key figure in the Catholic debate on whether or not non-Europeans, especially Native Americans, were to be saved and protected as human beings by the church. Fortunately for Native Americans, de las Casas prevailed, and the wholesale slaughter and enslavement of Indians was stopped, for a while. He also shows how the church was bound to temporal affairs, even in the New World. *Vasco da Gama*: unlike Cortés, the true explorer rather than conqueror. Da Gama was as interested in wealth as any other European, but his contributions were discovery and exploration rather than conquest and plunder.

14. Long before Columbus sailed, Europeans knew the world wasn't flat; Columbus was a brilliant, experienced cartographer and mariner, who was not looking for a new world, but rather an old one—a quicker water route to China and the East. Spain was interested in Columbus's plan, for they wanted to compete for the spice trade with their Iberian neighbor, Portugal. Most important, Columbus was not a great altruist, as once believed. Like all Europeans in the age of discovery, he was interested in wealth and fame. Whether or not he treated Native Americans with compassion and acceptance is moot; Columbus was an outstanding and daring seaman willing to risk much for discovery, wealth, and fame, and so he was like his contemporaries.

15. Answers should first include geographic location of respective empires, then discussion of their cultural, demographic, and religious differences. Aztecs regularly practiced human sacrifice; the Incas rarely did. Also, the Aztecs were a warrior society in perpetual conflict with their neighbors and in their empire. The Incas were less militaristic, had greater political stability as a result, and seemed more tolerant of other Amerindian cultures. Instead of human sacrifice, the Inca chiefs heavily taxed their subjects. Despite some differences, both of these great Amerindian empires were built on uneasy conquests. Subject groups would be willing allies for any invader.

Chapter 16
The Reformation

11. Selling "forgiveness of sins" was the final straw for many alienated Catholic clergy, who for years had watched the Catholic Church degenerate beyond redemption. Luther's condemnation of indulgences was just one of his ninety-nine grievances against the church, which he was convinced was corrupt from top to bottom.

12. Luther's message of biblical freedom carried a material as well as theological meaning. Peasants viewed material and religious life as the same. They argued that new tithes and taxes not only violated traditional feudal rights, but the Word of God. Inspired by Luther's theology, beginning in 1526, thousands of German peasants rose up against their seigneurial lords. Much to the peasants' dismay, Luther condemned their movements and urged that they be put down brutally.

13. Protestantism itself revitalized Catholicism. The Catholic response to the Protestant challenge was to reform the church from within. A new personal piety was stressed, which led to the founding of new spiritual orders, like the Jesuits (the Society of Jesus), who became the vanguard of the Catholic Counter-Reformation. The church hierarchy cared more about pastoral care and initiated reforms of the clergy at the parish level. The challenge of converting other races and bringing back fallen-away members led to missionary orders and new emphasis on preaching and education. The Catholic revival left Roman Catholicism stronger at the end of the era of religious reformation than it had been at the beginning.

14. To Calvin, providence guided all human behavior. Like Luther, Calvin accepted justification by faith alone and the biblical foundation of religious authority. He also believed like Luther and Zwingli that salvation came from God's grace, but more strongly than his predecessors he believed the gift of faith was granted only to some and that each individual's salvation or damnation was predestined before birth.

15. Both Lutheranism and Calvinism stripped man of free will—a concept the Catholic Church had reconciled long ago with Thomism. Salvation now was granted solely by God; with Calvin one was predestined for salvation or damnation, and no good works could alter God's will. Also the Bible took on a primacy that the Catholic Church had long since strayed from; they also minimized ritual and ceremony, as Protestant churches became austere places of worship. No saints were to be prayed to; no candles lit for God's "favor." No elaborate clerical hierarchy, only simple pastors who preached the Word to their congregations. Ministers and preachers were valuable because they could help others learn God's word, but they could not confer faith. Sin was ever present and inescapable. It could not be washed away by penance, and it could not be forgiven by indulgence. Finally, supposedly all who believed in God's righteousness were equal in God's eyes. Neither pope nor priest, monk nor nun could achieve higher spirituality than the most ordinary citizen.

Chapter 17
Europe in the Age of Philip II, 1559–1600

11. Great events of the sixteenth century—discovery of the New World, consolidation of states, increasing incidence and ferocity of war, religious reform and upheaval—all profoundly affected ordinary people. But these were not necessarily the most important transformations in people's lives. Continuity in family and community, and in daily customs and beliefs preserved orderliness and control of the natural environment. Most Europeans' lives were consumed by daily survival, births and deaths, the harvest, and social relations in their communities. The great events were the successful crop, marriage of an heir, or festivals marking the year's progress. Their beliefs were based as much on the customs they learned as children as on the religion they learned in church.

12. By the mid-sixteenth century, Spain was the greatest power in Europe. Philip II's dominions stretched from Atlantic to Pacific; his continental territories included the Netherlands in the north and Milan and Naples in Italy. In 1580, Philip became king of Portugal; yet over the next fifty years Spain's power declined rapidly. International warfare against the Turks and European conflicts with England, France, and the Netherlands revolt all drained money, men, and spirit from Europe's most powerful nation. Decades of warfare turned Spain's golden age to lead, hastening the decline of the Spanish empire.

13. *Nation-state*: England under Elizabeth I; *sovereignty*: the English Parliament; *balance of power*: English foreign policy toward the Continent. From these examples, extrapolate and correlate the concepts and definitions for each expression.

14. Civil wars tear the fabric of society, destroying institutions and the delicate relationships that underlie all communal life. The nation is divided; communities break into factions; families are destroyed. At every level of organization the glue that binds society comes unstuck. Civil wars are wars of passion. Passions run deep and rules for civilized conduct of war are quickly broken. Generations pass before societies recover from their civil wars, as with the French wars of religion. For nearly half a century civil war tore France apart. Massacres of Catholic congregations matched massacres of French Protestants. Assassinations of Catholic leaders followed assassinations of Protestants. Kings of France died at the hands of their subjects. The diverse elements of Calvinist zeal, monarchial weakness, and aristocratic ambition combined to cause the French civil war.

15. The international and civil wars in the sixteenth century were the impetus for much of the century's political thought. Incessant warfare caused the people to long for stability and order, to stop the wars and chaos. The people looked more and more to the monarchy as

the unifying agent rather than to traditional elites. In France, both Jean Bodin and Philippe du Plessis Mornay advanced theories making obedience to the king essential but conditional—he was to be obeyed as long as he acted for the common good. For both, ultimate state sovereignty rested with the monarchy. Such ideas envisioned an open-ended relationship between the ruler and the governed, rather than the government of traditional limits in the Medieval period.

Chapter 18
Europe in the Age of Louis XIV, 1610–1715

10. Beginning with the accession of James I, the monarchy was plunged into financial and political difficulties from which the Stuarts never escaped. Financial problems were the result of an undervalued tax base, making the monarchy increasingly dependent on extraordinary taxation grants that increased Parliament's power while creating political tension between Crown and Parliament. The first phase of this controversy resulted in the Petition of Right, promulgated in 1628 during the reign of Charles I. Religious problems mounted on top of economic and political difficulties. Tremendous pressure, especially from the Puritans, was put on the monarchy to make the Anglican church more Protestant—cleanse it of its still too Catholic liturgy and hierarchy. However, since the head of the Church of England was the king, an attack of the church was an attack on the monarchy. All of these tensions came to a violent head beginning in 1640 during the reign of Charles I, resulting finally in civil war in 1642. Conflict raged in England for five long years until finally parliamentary forces under Oliver Cromwell defeated Charles's royalists, and in 1649 Charles was executed for treason. Peace and stability returned to a weary England with the reign of Charles II, beginning in 1660. In 1685, however, Englishmen once again were confronted with the potential for revolution with the accession of James II, who was determined to rule England as an absolute monarch. Because of Parliament's victories some forty years earlier, that body had become sovereign and would not tolerate any encroachment on its supremacy. Parliament ousted James II in 1688 in a bloodless coup—the Glorious Revolution—thus preserving parliamentary sovereignty and avoiding civil war.

11. Louis's achievements include the consolidation of complete power in the monarchy; subduing the nobility; creating an efficient administrative bureaucracy and tax system; appointing energetic and dynamic ministers; reform of the French army, making it one of the largest and most powerful in Europe; and Louis himself—the epitome of the absolute monarch. Failures include an overaggressive foreign policy, which ultimately bankrupted the Crown; persecution of the Huguenots; harnessing the energies of the state of the purpose of the monarch, which required a level of wisdom and foresight that was not very common among monarchs or subjects.

12. Major causes: the Bohemian revolt, the defenestration of Prague, the resounding victory of Ferdinand II over the Protestant forces of the Holy Roman Empire, and the widening of the war to include Spain, France, Holland, Denmark, and Sweden. This was one of the most vicious and brutal wars in European history, exemplified by the Catholic victory at White Mountain and the Protestant victory at Magdeburg. Germany, especially, suffered greatly as its population declined by 4 million over the period of conflict. The rampaging armies brought destruction of all kinds in their wake, and plague and famine returned to Europe. Economies were buffeted by prolonged periods of inflation, devalued currency, and huge public and private debts. Finally, the war took an incalculable toll on the spirit of those generations that never knew peace.

13. Key factors were rivalry for colonial markets and empires, especially among the Dutch, English, and French; the discovery of precious metals (gold and silver) in the New World; the innovation, organization, and efficient management of the traders; the replacing of bilateral trade with triangular trade, which created a larger pool for desirable consumer goods; and changes made in the way trade was financed (giro banking, transfer system, etc.). The effects of these and many other smaller changes in business practices helped fuel prolonged growth in European commerce.

14. Demonstrate an understanding of French absolutism and the development of the monarchy versus the evolution of representative government in England. Students should emphasize that in both nations the evolution of the centralized state, regardless of where ultimate sovereignty rested, was an evolutionary process often entailing prolonged conflict.